GERMANY

PILGRIMAGE OF
UNITY AND PEACE

GERMANY
PILGRIMAGE OF UNITY AND PEACE

JOHN PAUL II

Compiled and Indexed
by the Daughters of St. Paul

ST. PAUL EDITIONS

Reprinted with permission from *L'Osservatore Romano*, English Edition.

Library of Congress Cataloging in Publication Data

John Paul II, Pope, 1920-
    Germany—pilgrimage of unity and peace.

    Speeches previously published in L'Osservatore romano, English ed.
    Includes index.
    1. Catholic Church—Addresses, essays, lectures.
2. Catholic Church—Sermons. 3. Sermons, English—Translations from German. 4. Sermons, German—Translations into English. I. Daughters of St. Paul.
II. Title.
BX891.J646   230'.2   81-2126
                             AACR2
ISBN 0-8198-3013-5 cloth
      0-8198-3014-3 paper

Photo credits:
Felici—119, 184, 225, 255, 261

Wide World—13, 17, 18, 25, 51, 75, 87, 131,
   135, 148, 193, 215, 264,
Arturo Mari—cover

Printed in the U.S.A. by the Daughters of St. Paul
50 St. Paul's Ave., Boston, MA 02130

The Daughters of St. Paul are an international congregation of religious women serving the Church with the communications media.

CONTENTS

"I COME TO YOU IN CHRIST'S NAME AS A FRIEND AND A BROTHER!"

On Saturday, November 15, the Holy Father began his pastoral visit to Germany. On his arrival at the Cologne-Bonn Airport, he was welcomed by the President of the Federal Republic of Germany. The Pope delivered the following address.

1. With deep interior emotion and gratitude towards divine Providence, which, with inscrutable will, has called me to Peter's See, I set foot today on German soil, whose people and country I have already gotten to know and appreciate personally on earlier visits.

I thank you sincerely, Mr. President of the Federal Republic, for your words of greeting which do me such honor, and from the bottom of my heart I return the expression of deep esteem with which, on behalf of your people, you have bid me welcome on my visit to the Federal Republic of Germany. At the same time I greet with you the personalities of political and social life present, the Diplomatic Corps represented here, and all the citizens of your country. My brotherly greeting goes in particular to the representatives of the Church, especially to His Eminence, Cardinal Joseph Höffner, so highly esteemed, while I express through him, to all pastors and faithful of the Catholic Church in Germany my deep attachment, affection and love.

2. I joyfully accepted the friendly invitation of the German Episcopal Conference and of the President of the Federal Republic of Germany for this visit to the country. As I already stressed in my announcement on August 10th of this year, I would like, with my pilgrimage to your country, to honor the whole great German nation, whose history is so closely linked with the history of Christianity and of the Church, and on which Christian tradition has imprinted such a deep stamp. In the course of the centuries many German men and women, with the example of their holiness, with their originality in the field of art and science, and in particular with deep philosophical reflection and theological research, have made a valuable contribution to the spiritual and cultural heritage of the Church and of the whole of humanity.

On this very day we are commemorating with the Church all over the world an eminent son of your country, who has also won the honorary title "Great": St. Albert the Great, the seventh centenary of whose death we are solemnly celebrating today. To bear witness to my special veneration for his venerable tomb and for the place of his last tireless activity is, as is known, the external occasion of my pilgrimage today. In him I honor at the same time the genius of the German people; I honor above all the Catholic Church of this country, which has remained up to our days, as in the past, such a respected and living member of the universal Church.

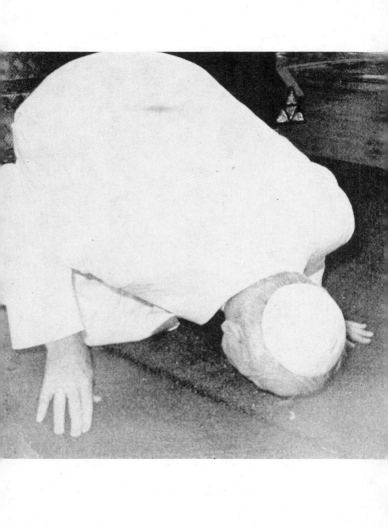

Its inspiring spiritual influence is still exercised today, not least of all with the competent collaboration of German bishops and theologians in the deliberations and decisions of the Second Vatican Council, in the life of the Church and far beyond the frontiers of this country.

The sense of responsibility of German Catholics extending beyond their local Church finds concrete expression, among other things, in the well-known great episcopal works of aid, in generous commitment for the missions, and in charitable activity for the needy all over the world. Therefore this visit of mine, linked with my three preceding apostolic pilgrimages in Third World countries (Mexico, Africa and Brazil), is intended to be also an expression of recognition and gratitude for the fact that the Church and the citizens of your country as a whole, in the spirit of universal brotherly solidarity, feel bound in this way to the needy populations of regions stricken by famine and disease, by natural catastrophies and human helplessness, and generously offer their aid and assistance.

3. But, as the aforesaid external occasion of my visit already emphasizes, my apostolic journey in the Federal Republic of Germany—like all the preceding ones—also has an exclusively pastoral and religious character. It regards, without any exception, all the men of this country, to whom I can come, in the name of Jesus Christ, as their friend and brother; it concerns particularly, however, my brothers and sisters in faith: the bishops, priests, religious, and the laity in their multiple fields of life and of work, all of whom I hope to meet individually during my five-day visit to the various places. At the same time I am anxious to greet all our separated brothers in faith. I am looking

forward to the personal meeting planned with the representatives responsible for their Churches and ecclesial Communities. God grant that my pilgrimage may contribute, beyond confessional boundaries, to greater mutual understanding and to a rapprochement among all Christians, and promote the peaceful coexistence of all men in this country. I have come here to the Federal Republic of Germany precisely in the year in which our evangelical brothers and sisters have commemorated the *Confessio Augustana*, proclaimed 450 years ago. Allow me to tell them that I particularly wanted to be among them at this very time. Here, where the Reformation began, may the effort also be redoubled to do, in fidelity to the one Lord of the Church and to His message, everything that is humanly possible, so that the desire of His heart and His prayer: "that they may all be one" (Jn. 17:21), may be fulfilled.

4. Through the mandate entrusted to me by the Lord, I know that I am sent in particular to the brothers and sisters of the Catholic Church of this country, to strengthen them in their faith and in their witness to the crucified and risen Christ, in the world of today, and to encourage them, before the growing challenge of an environment that is indifferent to religion, to respond with all the greater decision and courage to their Christian vocation and responsibility for making the family, professions, and society, more and more worthy of man.

With my pilgrimage today I return, in a way, the visit that such large numbers of German Catholics have already paid me during the first two years of my Pontificate at the weekly general audiences in the Vatican. Even though, for reasons of time, I can visit only some important places, I cordially invite also all believers and communities, particularly those brothers and sisters who, because of illness or other circumstances, are unable to participate personally, to join in spirit, through their prayer and sacrifice, the great praying community during the liturgical celebrations of the next few days. Through our common praise of God, in which we feel most deeply that we are the Church and realize her in living communion, may this memorable meeting of Peter's Successor with the People of God in the Federal Republic of Germany become, for all, days of grace and religious renewal. For this purpose, may St. Albert the Great implore for us assistance and blessings from God!

Once more I sincerely thank you, Mr. President, and all those who together with you honor me with their presence, for the friendly welcome and the cordial hospitality which you offer me in your country for the pastoral visit I am beginning.

God bless all Germans in the world!

God protect the Federal Republic of Germany!

THE KINGDOM OF GOD AND THE CHRISTIAN FAMILY

On Saturday, November 15, the Holy Father visited Cologne during his pilgrimage to Germany, his eighth such pilgrimage beyond the boundaries of Italy. His first Mass on German soil was celebrated in the sports arena of Butzweiler Hof. The Pope delivered the following homily.

1. "The kingdom of heaven is like a net..." (Mt. 13:47).

Allow me, Most Reverend Bishop of the ancient, venerable Church of Cologne, reverend confreres, Cardinals and bishops; allow me, all you beloved brothers and sisters, to try to clarify at this Eucharistic celebration the significance of our extraordinary meeting today, with the help of this parable, with the help of the Word of Christ, who repeatedly explained the kingdom of God by means of parables. With their help, He announced the presence of this kingdom in the midst of the world.

We, too, must meet in this dimension. This is, in a way, the essential premise of today's visit of the apostle Peter's Successor in the Episcopal See of Rome to your Church in Germany, to you here in

Cologne, who represent the Church of God as it has been formed in the course of many centuries round the Roman *Colonia Agrippina.* The outstanding symbol of this Church up to today has been your splendid cathedral, whose spiritual importance has been renewed in you, thanks to the jubilee this year: the latter speaks eloquently of the kingdom of God among us.

We who now form the Church of Christ on earth, on this part of the German territory, must meet in the dimension of the truth of the kingdom of God: Christ came to reveal this kingdom and launch it on this earth, in every place of the earth, in men and among men.

This kingdom of God is in our midst (cf. Lk. 17:21), as it was in all the generations of your fathers and ancestors. But like them, we too still pray in the "Our Father" every day: "Thy kingdom come." These words bear witness that the kingdom of God is still ahead of us, that we are moving towards it, advancing along the confused paths, and in fact sometimes even the wrong ones, of our earthly existence. We bear witness with these words that the kingdom of God is being continually realized and is approaching, even if we often lose sight of it and no longer see its form, described by the Gospel. It often seems that the one and only dimension of our existence is "this world": the "kingdom of this world" with its visible form, its breathtaking progress in science and technology, in culture and in economy...breathtaking and often also worrying! But if we kneel down to pray every day, or at least from time to time, we always utter, amid these circumstances of life, the same words: "Thy kingdom come."

Dear brothers and sisters! These hours in which we meet here, the time which, thanks to your invitation and your hospitality, I can spend among you, is *the time of the kingdom of God:* of the kingdom which is "already here," and of the one which is "still coming." For this reason we must interpret the whole essential part, which refers to this visit, with the help of the parable which we listen to in today's Gospel: "The kingdom of heaven is like...."

ANOTHER DIMENSION OF MAN'S EXISTENCE

2. What is it like?

According to the words of Jesus, as the four Evangelists transmitted them to us, this kingdom is explained with various parables and comparisons. Today's comparison is one of the many. It seems to us particularly closely connected with the work done by the Apostles of Christ, including Peter too, as well as by many of His listeners on the shores of the Sea of Galilee. Christ says: the kingdom of heaven is like "a net which was thrown into the sea and gathered fish of every kind" (Mt. 13:47). These simple words completely change the picture of the world: the picture of our human world, as we form it through experience and science. Experience and science cannot go beyond those boundaries of the "world" and of human existence in it, which are necessarily linked with the "sea of time": the boundaries of a world in which man is born and dies, in accordance with the words of Genesis: "You are dust, and to dust you shall return" (Gn. 3:1). The comparison of Christ, on the contrary,

We who now form the Church of Christ on earth, on this part of the German territory, must meet in the dimension of the truth of the kingdom of God: Christ came to reveal this kingdom and launch it on this earth, in every place of the earth, in men and among men.

speaks of man's transference into another "world," into another dimension of his existence. The kingdom of heaven is precisely this new dimension, which opens above the "sea of time" and is at the same time the "net" which works in this sea for the final destiny of man and of all men in God.

Today's parable calls upon us to recognize the kingdom of heaven as the *definitive fulfillment* of that *justice* for which man longs with invincible nostalgia, which the Lord has put in his heart; that justice which Jesus Himself realized and proclaimed; that justice, finally, which Christ sealed with His own blood on the cross.

In the kingdom of heaven, the kingdom "of justice, love and peace" (the Preface on the Feast of Christ the King), man, too, *will be perfect*. For man is the being who springs from the depth of God and himself conceals within him such a depth that only God can fill. He, man, is in all his being an image of God and is like Him.

FISHERS OF MEN

3. Jesus founded His Church on the twelve Apostles, several of whom were fishermen. The image of the net was very apropos. Jesus wanted to make them fishers of men. The Church, too, is a net, tied through the Holy Spirit, fastened through the apostolic mission, effective through unity in faith, life, and love.

I am thinking at this moment of the farspread net of the whole universal Church. At the same time, I see before my eyes every single Church in your land, especially the great Church of Cologne and the neighboring dioceses. And finally I see before my eyes the smallest of these Churches, the *"Ecclesiola,"* the domestic Church, to which the very recent Synod of Bishops in Rome gave such great attention in its subject on "the role of the Christian family."

The family: the domestic Church, the unique and irreplaceable community of persons, of which Saint Paul speaks in today's second reading. Here he has before his eyes, of course, the Christian family of his time; but what he says must also be applied to the problems of the families of our time: what he says to husbands, what he says to wives, to children and to parents. And finally *what he says to us all:* "Put on, then,...compassion, kindness, humility, meekness, and patience, forbearing one another and...forgiving each other.... And above all these put on love, which binds everything together in perfect harmony. And let the peace of Christ rule in your hearts, to which indeed you were called in the one body. And be thankful!" (Col. 3:12-15) What a great lesson of matrimonial and family spirituality!

REDISCOVER THE VALUE OF MARRIAGE

4. We, however, cannot close our eyes to the other side either; the Synod Fathers in Rome gave their earnest attention to it, too: I mean the difficulties to which the high ideal of the Christian concept of the family and of family life is exposed. Modern industrial society has fundamentally changed the conditions of life for marriage and the family. Marriage and the family were previously not only communities of life, but also communities of production and economy. They have been ousted from many public

functions. Public opinion is not always favorable to marriage and the family. And yet, in our anonymous mass civilization, they prove to be a place of refuge in the search for a haven and happiness. Marriage and the family are more important than ever: cells of reproduction for the renewal of society, springs of strength, because of which life becomes more human. I can draw inspiration from the image: the net, which gives support and unity and raises from the currents of the deep.

Let us not allow this net to break. The state and society are on the way to their own decline if they do not support marriage and the family more effectively, and do not protect them more, and if they put them on the same level as other non-matrimonial communities of life. All men of good will, particularly we Christians, are called to rediscover the dignity and value of marriage and the family and to live them before men in a convincing way. The Church, with the light of faith, offers her advice and her spiritual service for this purpose.

PERSONAL BOND OF FIDELITY

5. Marriage and the family are very deeply connected with man's personal dignity. They are not derived only from instinct and passion, nor only from feeling; they are derived in the first place from a decision of the free will, from a personal love, because of which spouses become not only one flesh, but also one heart and one soul. Physical and sexual communion is something great and beautiful. But it is fully worthy of man only if it is integrated in a personal union, recognized by the civil and ecclesiastical com-

munity. Full sexual communion between man and woman is legitimate, therefore, only within the exclusive and definitive personal bond of fidelity in marriage. The indissolubility of conjugal fidelity, which is no longer understandable to many people today, is likewise an expression of man's unconditional dignity. One cannot live only on trial, one cannot die only on trial. One cannot love only on trial, accept a person only on trial and for a limited time.

THE RIGHT TO LIFE

6. Thus marriage is geared to duration, to the future. It looks beyond itself. Marriage alone is suitable for procreation and the upbringing of children. Therefore, matrimonial love is by its very nature geared also to fertility. In this role of handing down life, spouses are collaborators with the love of God the Creator. I know that here, too, in today's society, the difficulties are great. Burdens, particularly for the woman. Small houses, economic and health problems, and often even a declared prejudice against large families, are an obstacle to greater fertility. I appeal to all those responsible, to all forces of society: do everything to bring help. I appeal first of all, however, to your conscience and to your personal responsibility, dear brothers and sisters. You must make the decision about the number of your children in your conscience, in the presence of God.

As spouses you are called to responsible parenthood. This, however, means a family planning that respects ethical norms and criteria, as was also stressed by the recent Synod of Bishops. In this connection I wish to recall emphatically to your memory today only the following: the killing of unborn life is not a legitimate means of family planning. I repeat what I said on May 31 of this year to workers in the Parisian suburb of Saint-Denis: "The first right of man is the right to life. We must defend this right and this value. In the contrary case, the whole logic of faith in man, the whole program of really human progress, would be shaken and collapse."

As a matter of fact, it is a question of this: to serve life.

MYSTERY OF MARRIAGE AND THE FAMILY

7. Dear brothers and sisters! On the indispensable foundation and premises of what has been said, we wish to turn now to the deepest mystery of marriage and the family. From the point of view of our faith, marriage is a sacrament of Jesus Christ. Love and conjugal fidelity are understood and sustained by the love and fidelity of God in Jesus Christ. The power of His cross and of His resurrection sustains and sanctifies Christian spouses.

As the recent Synod of Bishops stressed in its Message to Christian Families in the Modern World, the Christian family is called in particular to collaborate in God's salvific plan, since it helps its members "to become agents of the history of salvation and at the same time living signs of God's loving plan for the world" (Sect. III, no. 8).

As a "Church in miniature," sacramentally founded, or domestic Church, marriage and the family must be a school of faith and a place of common prayer. I attribute great significance precisely to prayer in the family. It gives strength to overcome the many problems and difficulties. In marriage and in the family, the fundamental human and Christian attitudes, without which the Church and society cannot exist, must grow and mature. This is the first place for the Christian apostolate of the laity and of the common priesthood of all the baptized. Such marriages and families, imbued with the Christian spirit, are also the real seminaries, that is, seedbeds for spiritual vocations for the priestly and religious states.

Dear spouses and parents, dear families! What could I more heartily wish you on the occasion of today's Eucharistic meeting than this: that all of you and every single family may be such a "domestic Church," a Church in miniature! That the parable of the kingdom of God may be realized in you! That you may experience the presence of the kingdom of God, in that you are yourselves a living "net," which unites and supports and gives refuge for yourselves and for many around you.

This is my good wish and blessing, which I express as your guest and pilgrim and as the servant of your salvation.

REFLECTION ON
SAINT ALBERT THE GREAT

8. And now allow me, at the end of this fundamental reflection on the kingdom of God and on the Christian family, to turn again to St. Albert the Great, the celebration of whose seventh centenary has brought me to your city. Here, in fact, is the tomb of this famous son of your country, who was born in Lauingen, and in his long life was at once a great

scientist, a spiritual son of St. Dominic, and the teacher of St. Thomas Aquinas. He was one of the greatest intellects of the 13th century. More than any other, he wove the "net" that unites faith and reason, God's wisdom and worldly knowledge. At least in spirit I also visit the city in which he was born, Lauingen, while today, here in Cologne, close to his tomb, I stop to meditate together with you on the words with which today's liturgy celebrates him:

"If the great Lord is willing,
he will be filled with the spirit of understanding;
he will pour forth words of wisdom
and give thanks to the Lord in prayer.
He will direct his counsel and knowledge aright,
and meditate on his secrets.
He will reveal instruction in his teaching,
and will glory in the law of the Lord's covenant.
Many will praise his understanding, and it will never
    be blotted out;
his memory will not disappear, and his name will live
    through all generations.
Nations will declare his wisdom, and the congrega-
    tion will proclaim his praise" (Sir. 39:6-10).

There is nothing to be added to these words of the wise son of Sirach. But neither must any be left out. They describe perfectly, in fact, the figure of that man on whom your country, your city, rightly pride themselves, and who is a joy for the whole Church. *Albertus Magnus, doctor universalis*—Albert the Great, of vast learning: a real "disciple of the kingdom of God"! If we have reflected together today on the vocation of the Christian family to build up the kingdom of God on earth, the words of Christ's parable must also give us the deepest significance of this saint, whom we are solemnly commemorating today. Christ says, in fact: "Every scribe who has been trained for the kingdom of heaven is like a householder who brings out of his treasure what is new and what is old" (Mt. 13:52).

St. Albert, too, is like this householder! May his example and his intercession accompany me, while I try on my pilgrimage through your country, as a fisher of men, to knot the net more tightly and throw it out further, in order that the kingdom of God may come. Amen.

APPEAL FOR KIDNAPPED GIRL

Before continuing with the liturgical celebration, I am deeply concerned in the context of today's meditation on marriage and the family, to express on behalf of you all my emotion at the cruel kidnapping of an eleven-year-old girl, Cornelia Becker, which has just taken place in your country. We share the apprehension of the parents for the fate of their daughter. Once more we feel to our grief what human aberration and ruthlessness are capable of. In the name of humanity I appeal to the conscience of the kidnappers: desist from your inhuman action! Release the innocent child Cornelia immediately! We now wish to address in prayer this supplication to God, who has access to men's hearts, where our words do not arrive. Let us pray with the anxious parents for a joyful reunion with their daughter soon. Lord Jesus Christ, You are the truth. Listen to our supplication. Amen.

PRAYER AT THE TOMB OF ST. ALBERT THE GREAT

November 15, 1980: Church of St. Andrew, Cologne.

God, You are wondrous in Your saints!

Appointed by You to the highest pastoral office of the Church of Jesus Christ, I kneel today as a pilgrim at the tomb of St. Albert, to glorify You with all the faithful on this day commemorating the 700th anniversary of his death, and to thank You for his life and his works, through which You gave him to Your Church as a teacher of the faith and an example of Christian life.

God, our Creator, cause and light of the human spirit, You gave St. Albert a profound knowledge of faith in true imitation of our Lord and Master Jesus Christ. The world itself became for him the revelation of Your omnipotence and goodness. Through his contact with Your creation he learned to recognize and love You more profoundly. At the same time he researched through the works of human wisdom, including the writings of non-Christian philosophers, and paved the way for their encounter with Your

Gospel. Through the gift of discrimination You made him uniquely able to avoid error, to establish truth more deeply and make it known among men. In doing so You made him a teacher of the Church and of all mankind.

With the intercession of St. Albert we pray together to You for Your mercy:

—Send to Your Church teachers of truth in our time as well, who will be capable of interpreting and preaching Your Gospel to the people of the world through their words and saintly living. Hear us, O Lord.

—Open the hearts of men through the grace of a living faith so that they may recognize God's presence in His creation and their own lives and come to correspond more and more perfectly with His holy will.

—Accompany and illuminate the work of scientists and scholars with Your Holy Spirit. Preserve them from pride and self-conceit and give them a sense of responsibility in their dealings with the gifts of Your creation.

—Give those responsible in state and society insight and responsibility so that they may use the achievements of science and technology for peace and progress among the peoples of the world and not for their harm or destruction.

—Help us all to recognize the truth amidst the many dangers and errors of our time and to serve You devoutly in a life strengthened by faith.

—With the intercession of St. Albert bless all citizens of this country, give the German people peace and unity and let it always be aware of its responsibility in the community of nations.

—Accompany my pastoral visit in the Federal Republic of Germany with Your special blessings and assistance. Strengthen all believers in their love of Christ and His Church so that through the testimony of their Christian living Your name may be glorified in truth and justice in the world today.

Pray for us, St. Albert, that we might be worthy of the promises of Christ.

Let us pray: God, our refuge and strength, You gave the sainted bishop and teacher of the Church, Albert, the power to associate human knowledge with eternal wisdom. With his intercession, strengthen and protect our faith in the intellectual confusion of our days. Give us the openness of his intellect so that the progress of science may also help us to know You more profoundly and come closer to You. Let us grow in the knowledge of the truth which You Yourself are, so that we may someday see You face to face in the presence of all the saints. For this we pray through Christ our Lord. Amen.

CONNECTION BETWEEN SCIENTIFIC THOUGHT AND THE POWER OF FAITH IN THE SEARCH FOR TRUTH

In the early afternoon of Saturday, November 15, John Paul II met teachers and university students in Cologne Cathedral. During the meeting the Holy Father delivered the following address.

Venerable confrères in the Episcopate!
Beloved brothers and sisters!
Ladies and gentlemen!

1. I greet you with joy and gratitude, men and women scientists of the Federal Republic of Germany, students of the German universities, which have exercised such a lasting influence on the history of science in Europe. You are gathered here also as representatives of the many researchers, teachers, collaborators and students in the universities, academies and other research institutes. You also represent the numerous collaborators who, engaged in research in the public and private sectors, exercise

a considerable influence on the development of science and technology, and consequently have a particular responsibility with regard to men.

SIGN OF READINESS FOR DIALOGUE

2. Today's meeting must be understood as a sign of readiness for dialogue between science and the Church. The day itself, as well as the place, gives this meeting special importance. Seven hundred years ago today, there died in a Dominican convent not far from this cathedral, at whose foundation he was probably present, Albert "the German," as his contemporaries called him, and on whom, alone among the doctors of the Church, posterity conferred the title "the Great."

Albert carried out a multiple activity in his time as a religious and a preacher, as religious superior, as bishop and mediator of peace in his own city, Cologne. But his claim to fame in world history is as a researcher and scholar who mastered the knowledge of his time and made it his lifework to reorganize it. His contemporaries already recognized in him the *auctor*, the initiator and promoter of science. Posterity defined him as *doctor universalis*. The Church, which counts him among her saints, refers to him as one of her "doctors" and honors him in the liturgy under this title.

Our memory of Albert the Great, however, must not be just an act of due piety. It is more important to actualize again the essential meaning of his lifework, to which we must attribute a fundamental and abiding importance. Let us cast a brief glance at the historico-cultural situation of Albert's time. It is marked by the growing rediscovery of Aristotelian literature and of Arabic science. Up to then the Christian West had kept alive and scientifically developed the tradition of Christian antiquity.

Now it is met by a comprehensive non-Christian view of the world, based only on a profane rationality. Many Christian thinkers, including some very important ones, saw above all a danger in this claim. They thought they had to defend the historical identity of Christian tradition against it; for there were also radical individuals and groups who saw an unsolvable conflict between scientific rationality and the truth of faith, and made their choice in favor of this "scientific precedence."

Between these two extremes Albert takes the middle way: the claim to truth of a science based on rationality is recognized; in fact, it is accepted in its contents, completed, corrected and developed in its independent rationality. And precisely in this way it becomes the property of the Christian world. In this way the latter sees its own understanding of the world enormously enriched without having to give up any essential element of its tradition, far less the foundation of its faith. For there can be no fundamental conflict between a reason which, in conformity with its own nature which comes from God, is geared to truth and is qualified to know truth, and a faith, which refers to the same divine source of all truth. Faith confirms, in fact, the specific rights of natural reason. It presupposes them. In fact, its acceptance presupposes that freedom which is characteristic only of a rational being. This shows at the same time that faith and science belong to different orders of knowledge, which cannot be transferred from one to the other. It is seen, furthermore, that reason cannot do everything alone; it is finite. It must proceed through a multiplicity of separate branches of knowledge; it is composed of a plurality of individual sciences. It can grasp the unity which binds the world and truth with their origin only within partial ways of knowledge. Also philosophy and theology are, as sciences, limited attempts which can represent the complex unity of truth only in diversity, that is, within an open system of complementary items of knowledge.

Let us repeat: Albert recognizes the articulation of rational science in a system of different branches of knowledge in which it finds confirmation of its own peculiarity, and at the same time remains geared to the goals of faith. In this way Albert realizes the statute of a Christian intellectuality, whose fundamental principles are still to be considered valid today. We do not diminish the importance of this achievement if we affirm at the same time: Albert's work is from the point of view of content bound to his own time and therefore belongs to history. The "synthesis" he made retains an exemplary character, and we would do well to call to mind its fundamental principles when we turn to the present-day questions about science, faith, and the Church.

IN FAVOR OF FREEDOM OF RESEARCH

3. Many people see the core of these questions in the relationship between the Church and modern natural sciences, and they still feel the weight of those notorious conflicts which arose from the interference of religious authorities in the process of the development of scientific knowledge. The Church remembers this with regret, for today we realize the errors and

shortcomings of these ways of proceeding. We can say today that they have been overcome: thanks to the power of persuasion of science, and thanks above all to the work of a scientific theology, which has deepened understanding of faith and freed it from the conditionings of time. The ecclesiastical Magisterium has, since the First Vatican Council, recalled those principles several times, most recently and explicitly in the Second Vatican Council *(Gaudium et spes,* no. 36), principles which are already recognizable in the work of Albert the Great. It has explicitly affirmed the distinction of orders of knowledge between faith and reason; it has recognized the autonomy and independence of science, and has taken up a position in favor of freedom of research. We do not fear, in fact we deny, that a science which is based on rational motives and proceeds with methodological seriousness can arrive at knowledge which is in conflict with the truth of faith. This can happen only when the distinction of the orders of knowledge is neglected or denied.

This view, which should be ratified by scientists, could help to overcome the historical weight of the relationship between Church and science, and facilitate a dialogue on an equal footing, as already often happens in practice. It is not just a question of overcoming the past, but of new problems, which derive from the role of sciences in universal culture today.

RADICAL TRANSFORMATION IN TECHNOLOGY

Scientific knowledge has led to a radical transformation of human technology. Consequently, the conditions of human life on this earth have changed enormously and have also considerably improved. The progress of scientific knowledge has become the driving power of general cultural progress. The transformation of the world at the technical level seemed to many people to be the meaning and purpose of science. In the meantime, it has been seen that the progress of civilization does not always improve living conditions. There are involuntary and unexpected consequences, which may become dangerous and harmful. I will recall only the ecological problem, which arose as a result of the progress of technico-scientific industrialization. In this way serious doubts arise as to whether progress, on the whole, serves man. These doubts have repercussions on science, understood in the technical sense. Its meaning, its aim, its human significance are questioned.

This question takes on particular weight with regard to the use of scientific thought regarding man. The so-called human sciences have supplied extremely important information concerning human activity and behavior. They run the risk, however, in a culture determined by technology, to be misused in order to manipulate man, for purposes of economic and political domination.

If science is understood essentially as "a technical fact," then it can be conceived as the pursuit of those processes that lead to technical success. What leads to success, therefore, is considered "knowledge." The world, at the level of a scientific datum, becomes a mere complex of phenomena that can be manipulated, and the object of science a functional connection, which is examined only with reference to its functionality. Such a science may conceive itself as a mere function. The concept of truth, therefore, becomes superfluous, and sometimes, in fact, it is explicitly renounced. Reason itself seems, when all is said and done, a mere function or an instrument of a being who finds the meaning of his existence outside knowledge and science, if possible in mere life.

FACING ITS OWN LIMITS

Our culture, in all its areas, is imbued with a science which proceeds in a way that is largely functionalistic. This applies also to the area of values and norms, of spiritual orientation in general. Precisely here science comes up against its own limits. There is talk of a crisis of legitimation of science, nay more, of a crisis of orientation of our whole scientific culture. What is its essence? Science alone is not able to give a complete answer to the question of meanings, which is raised in the crisis. Scientific affirmations are always particular. They are justified only in consideration of a given starting point, they are set in a process of development, and they can be corrected and left behind in this process. But above all: how could something constitute the result of a scientific starting point when it first justifies this starting point and therefore must already be presupposed by it?

Science alone is not capable of answering the question of meanings; in fact, it cannot even set it in the framework of its starting point. And yet, this question of meanings cannot tolerate indefinite postponement of its answer. If widespread confidence in science is disappointed, then the state of mind easily changes into hostility to science. In this space that has remained empty, ideologies suddenly break in. They sometimes behave as if they were "scientific," but they owe their power of persuasion to the urgent need for an answer to the question of meanings and to interest in social and political change. Science that is purely functional, without values and alienated from truth, can enter the service of these ideologies; a reason that is only instrumental runs the risk of losing its freedom. Finally, there are new manifestations of superstition, sectarianism, and the so-called "new religions," whose appearance is closely connected with the crisis of orientation of culture.

These wrong ways can be detected and avoided by faith. But the common crisis concerns also the believing scientist. He will have to ask himself in what spirit, in what direction, he is pursuing his studies. He must assume the task, directly or indirectly, of examining, in a constantly renewed form, the procedure and aim of science from the standpoint of the question of meanings. We are jointly responsible for this culture and we are called upon to cooperate in overcoming the crisis.

4. In this situation the Church does not advocate prudence and restraint, but courage and decision.

There is no reason not to take up a position in favor of truth or to be afraid of it. The truth and everything that is true represents a great good to which we must turn with love and joy. Science, too, is a way to truth; for God's gift of reason—which according to its nature is destined not for error, but for the truth of knowledge—is developed in it.

This must apply also to science orientated in a technico-functional direction. It is reductive to understand knowledge only as a "method for success," while on the contrary it is legitimate to judge as a proof of knowledge the outcome it obtains. We cannot consider the technical world, the work of man, as a kingdom completely estranged from truth. Then, too, this world is anything but meaningless: it is true that it has decisively improved living conditions, and the difficulties caused by the harmful effects of the development of technical civilization do not justify forgetting the goods that this same progress has brought.

There is no reason to consider technico-scientific culture as opposed to the world of God's creation. It is clear beyond all doubt that technical knowledge can be used for good as well as for evil. Anyone who studies the effects of poison can use this knowledge to cure as well as to kill. But there can be no doubt in what direction we must look to distinguish good from evil.

Technical science, aimed at the transformation of the world, is justified on the basis of the service it renders man and humanity.

It cannot be said that progress has gone too far as long as many people, in fact whole peoples, still live in distressing conditions, unworthy of man, which could be improved with the help of technico-scientific knowledge. Enormous tasks still lie before us, which we cannot shirk. To carry them out represents a brotherly service for our neighbor, to whom we owe this commitment, just as we owe the man in need the work of charity, which helps his necessity.

We render our neighbor a brotherly service because we recognize in him that dignity char-acteristic of a moral being; we are speaking of personal dignity. Faith teaches us that man's fundamental prerogative consists in being the image of God. Christian tradition adds that man is of value for his own sake, and is not a means for any other end. Therefore man's personal dignity represents the criterion by which all cultural application of technico-scientific knowledge must be judged.

REPERCUSSIONS IN PRIVATE AND PUBLIC LIFE

This is of particular importance at a time when man is becoming more and more the object of research and of human technologies. It is not yet a question of an unlawful way of proceeding, because man is also "nature." Certainly, dangers and problems arise here, which, due to the worldwide effects of technical civilization, raise completely new tasks for most peoples today. These dangers and problems have been for a long time the subject of discussion at the international level. It is a proof of the high sense of responsibility .of modern science that it takes charge of these fundamental problems and endeavors to solve them with scientific means.

The human and social sciences, but also the sciences of culture, not least of all philosophy and theology, have stimulated in multiple ways the reflection of modern man about himself and his existence in a world dominated by science and technology. The spirit of modern consciousness, which accelerates the development of the modern natural sciences, has also set for itself as its purpose the scientific analysis of man and of the world in which he lives, at the social and cultural level. An absolutely incalculable mass of knowledge has thereby come to light, which has repercussions on both public and private life. The social system of modern states, the health and educational system, economic processes and cultural activities are all marked in many ways by the influence of these sciences. But it is important that science should not keep man under its thumb. Also in the culture of technology, man, in conformity with his dignity, must remain free; in fact, it must be the meaning of this culture to give him greater freedom.

It is not only faith that offers the perception of man's personal dignity and of its decisive importance. Natural reason, too, can have access to it, since it is able to distinguish truth from falsehood, good from evil, and recognizes freedom as the fundamental condition of human existence. It is an encouraging sign, which is spreading all over the world. The concept of human rights does not mean anything else, and not even those who, in actual fact, oppose it with their actions, can escape it. There is hope, and we want to encourage this hope.

More and more voices are raised that refuse to be content with the immanent limitation of sciences and ask about a complete truth in which human life is fulfilled. It is as if knowledge and scientific research stretched out towards the infinite, only to snap back to their origins: the old problem of the connection between science and faith has not become outdated with the development of modern sciences; on the contrary, in a world more and more imbued with science, it manifests its full vital importance.

KNOWLEDGE OF TRUTH
HAS ITS MEANING

5. We have spoken so far mainly of the science that is in the service of culture and consequently of man. It would be too little, however, to limit ourselves to this aspect. Precisely with regard to the crisis, we must remember that science is not only service for other purposes. Knowledge of truth has its meaning in itself. It is an accomplishment of human and personal character, an outstanding human good. Pure "theory" is itself a kind of human "praxis," and the believer is waiting for a supreme "praxis," which will unite him forever with God: that "praxis" which is vision, and therefore also "theory."

We have spoken of the "crisis of the legitimation of science." Certainly, science has a meaning of its own and a justification when it is recognized as being capable of knowing truth, and when truth is recognized as a human good. Then also the demand for the freedom of science is justified; in what way, in fact, could a human good be realized if not through freedom? Science must be free also in the sense that its implementation must not be determined by direct purposes of social utility or economic interest. That does not mean, however, that on principle it must be separated from "praxis." But to be able to influence "praxis," it must first be determined by truth, and therefore be free for truth.

A free science, bound only to truth, does not let itself be reduced to the model of functionalism or any other, which limits understanding of scientific rationality. Science must be open; in fact, it must also be multiform, and we need not fear the loss of a unified approach. This is given by the trinomial of personal reason, freedom and truth, in which the multiplicity of concrete realizations is founded and confirmed.

I do not hesitate at all to see also the science of faith on the horizon of rationality understood in this way. The Church wants independent theological research, which is not identified with the ecclesiastical Magisterium, but which knows it is committed with regard to it in common service of the truth of faith and the People of God. It cannot be ignored that tensions and even conflicts may arise. But this cannot be ignored either as regards the relationship between Church and science. The reason is to be sought in the finiteness of our reason, limited in its extension and therefore exposed to error. Nevertheless we can always hope for a solution of reconciliation, if we take our stand on the ability of this same reason to attain truth.

THE CHURCH MUST TAKE UP DEFENSE

In the past, precursors of modern science fought against the Church with the slogans: reason, freedom and progress. Today, in view of the crisis with regard to the meaning of science, the multiple threats to its freedom and the doubt about progress, the battle fronts have been inverted. Today it is the Church that takes up the defense:

—for reason and science, which she recognizes as having the ability to attain truth, which legitimizes it as a human realization;

—for the freedom of science, through which the latter possesses its dignity as a human and personal good;

—for progress in the service of a humanity which needs it to safeguard its life and its dignity.

With this task, the Church and all Christians are at the center of the debate of these times of ours. An adequate solution of the pressing questions about the meaning of human existence, norms of action, and the prospects of a more far-reaching hope, is possible only in the renewed connection between scientific thought and the power of faith in man in search of truth. The pursuit of a new humanism on which the future of the third millennium can be based, will be successful only on the condition that scientific knowledge again enters upon a living relationship with the truth revealed to man as God's gift. Man's reason is a grand instrument for knowledge and structuring of the world. It needs, however, in order to realize the whole wealth of human possibilities, to open to the Word of eternal truth, which became man in Christ.

OBJECTIVELY AND PERSEVERINGLY

I said at the beginning that our meeting today was to be a sign of the readiness for dialogue between science and the Church. Has it not emerged clearly from these reflections how urgent this dialogue is? Both parties must continue it objectively, listening to each other, and perseveringly. We need each other.

In this cathedral there have been kept and venerated for centuries the bones of the Wise Men, who at the beginning of the new age which dawned with the Incarnation of God, set out to pay homage to the true Lord of the world. These men, in whom the knowl-

Man's reason is a grand instrument for knowledge and structuring of the world. It needs, however, in order to realize the whole wealth of human possibilities, to open to the Word of eternal truth, which became man in Christ.

edge of their time was summed up, become, therefore, the model of every man in search of truth. The knowledge which reason attains finds its completion in the adoration of divine Truth. The man who sets out towards this Truth does not suffer any loss of his freedom: on the contrary, in trusting dedication to the Spirit whom we have been promised through Jesus Christ's redeeming work, he is led to complete freedom and to the fullness of a truly human existence.

I appeal to the scientists, students, and·all of you gathered here today, and ask you always to keep before your eyes, in your striving for scientific knowledge, the ultimate aim of your work and of your whole life. For this purpose I recommend to you particularly the virtues of courage, which defends science in a world marked by doubt, alienated from truth, and in need of meaning; and humility, through which we recognize the finiteness of reason before truth which transcends it. These are the virtues of Albert the Great.

PRAYER AT THE TOMBS OF DUNS SCOTUS AND ADOLPH KOLPING

After a short stop for prayer at the tombs of Duns Scotus and Mons. Kolping, in the church of the Conventual Friars Minor in Cologne, the Holy Father addressed the Kolping community in the afternoon of Saturday, November 15, as follows.

Dear Kolping community!

The cathedral from which I have just come has two mighty towers, which soar into the sky like witnesses to faith. The church of the Friars Minor, of the same age as the cathedral, embraces two spiritual towers of faith: the important theologian, Duns Scotus, and the great social pastor of the people, Adolph Kolping. Duns Scotus revealed to us the secret of Mary's Immaculate Conception and described her position in God's plan of salvation. This house of God was the first one north of the Alps to be consecrated to Mary Immaculate. Beside the thinker there rests in this church the pastor, popular writer and social apostle, Adolph Kolping.

Adolph Kolping called for new reflection by man on his inner value, given by God, in the family, in his profession, in the Church, in the state, and in society. His program runs: Every single Christian changes the world if he lives in a Christian way. Adolph Kolping lived in a period of political and social upheaval. He knew that the individual, in isolation, could contribute but little to the improvement of relationships. Therefore, he zealously built up the Catholic Unions, now the International Kolping Work. His aim was to offer shelter and a home to men in a difficult social situation.

When Adolph Kolping founded his first social unions in Cologne, Karl Marx, too, was operating there. The latter called for revolution and the class struggle; Adolph Kolping wished to change society through the Christian behavior of men. The foundations of his work were the message of Christ and Catholic social doctrine, which he spread by means of his writings, and to which he gave impetus. I have come to thank Adolph Kolping and Kolping's International Work, which carries out his program adapted to the requirements of the time, for their contribution to the solution of social problems. I have heard to my great joy that today Kolping's Work has spread to 20 nations of the earth, and that recently it has been spreading in a very beneficial way also in the Third World. I am particularly happy that so many young people join your Work everywhere and let themselves be formed by it, to behave in a way that bears witness to the Good News entrusted to them.

I know of your great desire for the beatification of Father Kolping. I wish to encourage you in this and to bless your efforts. I repeat what I already said here in 1978: "For the Church of today we need leading figures such as Adolph Kolping."

"PEACE BE WITHIN YOUR WALLS"

Arriving on Saturday evening at Bonn, the second stage of his apostolic pilgrimage in the Federal Republic of Germany, the Holy Father stopped briefly in front of the cathedral, where he delivered the following address to the many persons present.

Praised be Jesus Christ!

I thank you heartily, dear brothers and sisters, for having prepared, at such a late hour, such a cordial welcome in your city of Bonn for me, the apostolic pilgrim through your land. I greet those who are present and all the inhabitants of the Federal Republic with the psalmist's words of blessing: "Peace be within your walls.... For my brethren and companions' sake I will say, Peace be within you!" (Ps. 121-122) My greeting goes in particular to the supreme representatives of the civil and ecclesial community, to the city's mayor and dean. At the same time I greet the representatives of the Christian Churches and of the Jewish community.

Your venerable cathedral basilica, where we here meet, treasures in its crypt the tombs of the patron saints of your city, the holy Roman martyrs, Cassius and Florentius. This early monument of Christianity always reminds you of the Christian roots of your city and your culture. The heroic profession of Christ by these two witnesses of faith, whose feast day you celebrate so solemnly every year with the municipal council of the city, lays an obligation upon you. You, too, be such convinced and convincing Christians today! May the present renewal of your magnificent house of God be an appeal to you. We, too, the living stones of the spiritual temple of the Church, must always renew ourselves in Jesus Christ, until we are fully conformed to Him.

"For the sake of the house of the Lord our God, I will seek your good" (Ps. 122:9). With these words of the same psalm I implore the perennial protection and blessing of God for your city and for all its inhabitants. God bless the families with their children! God bless the old! God bless those who are ill in bed! God bless anyone who feels lonely, who is full of worries and disheartened!

Finally our special blessing in this capital of the Federal Republic goes to all those who bear heavy responsibility for the political fate and welfare of your people and the international community of people. May God illuminate their consultations and decisions with His light!

Let us now pray for your city, for your people, and for the whole Church, as the Lord taught us to pray:

Our Father who art in heaven....

ALL TRUE PROGRESS SERVES THE ENTIRE MAN

The official meeting of the Holy Father with the authorities of the Federal Republic of Germany took place in the late evening of Saturday, November 15, at Brühl Castle. After the private meeting with the President of the Republic and with Chancellor Schmidt, the Holy Father delivered the following address, in the presence of the highest authorities of the Republic, in reply to the greeting of President Karl Carstens.

Mr. President of the Federal Republic,
Mr. President of the Chamber,
Mr. Federal Chancellor,
Venerable confrères in the episcopate,
Ladies and gentlemen,

1. It is a special joy for me, during my visit in the Federal Republic of Germany, to be able to meet you, the highest and authoritative representatives of the political, cultural, economic, and religious life of this nation. In you I greet at the same time all those who bear responsibility in this country for the welfare and the destiny of the whole people.

I sincerely thank the President of the Federal Republic for his friendly greeting of welcome, and all of you who honor me with your presence. Your attention, which I appreciate, certainly goes not so much to my capacity as Sovereign of the Vatican State, of such modest external dimensions, as to the religious mission entrusted to me as the Supreme Pastor of the Catholic Church. This alone causes me to leave the Eternal City time and again for a few days, in the spirit of my great Predecessors in Peter's See and in accordance with the new pastoral needs of our time, to pay a pastoral visit to my brothers and sisters in faith in the various local Churches and continents.

EXPRESSION OF SOLIDARITY

2. My meetings with the highest public and civil authorities during my apostolic journeys are intended to be not only gestures of courtesy and esteem, but are at the same time the expression of the solidarity and co-responsibility to which the Church knows she is committed by virtue of her mission—taking into account the existing circumstances—together with the state for the common good of citizens, although the aim given by Christ to the Church belongs to another order, namely the religious one, as the Second Vatican Council stresses, "this religious mission can be the source of commitment, direction and vigor to establish and consolidate the community of men according to the law of God" (*Gaudium et spes*, no. 42).

The history of your people and of the whole Christian West is rich in shining examples and valuable results of such a co-responsible and trustful collaboration between the state, society, and the Church. Eloquent testimonies of how the power of faith and the organization of the world are connected, are not only the splendid cathedrals, the venerable cloisters and universities with their vast libraries, and the many other cultural and social institutions, but

also modern technical civilization and culture themselves, which cannot be understood without the
decisive historical, spiritual, and moral contribution
of Christianity since their origins. Even modern
areligious and antireligious ideologies still bear
witness to the existence and high value of what they
endeavor to deny and destroy with all means.

GERMANY'S CONTRIBUTION

3. Because of its significant spiritual-religious,
cultural, and scientific contribution, special recognition is due to the German people in the history of
the Church and in the spiritual history of Europe. In
its past there are certainly lights and shadows, as in
the life of every nation, examples of the highest human and Christian greatness, but also abysses, trials,
deeply tragic events. There are times in which the life
of this nation corresponded to true human and Christian virtue, but there are also times that were in contradiction with the latter in civil and international
life. But your country has always been able to rise
again even from ruin and humiliations—as for example those of the last World War—and acquire new
strength. Political stability, technical and scientific
progress, and the proverbial diligence of the citizens
have enabled the Federal Republic of Germany in the
last few decades to achieve prosperity and social
peace within its own boundaries, and beyond them
high prestige and influence in the international community of peoples. There has still remained for your
people, however, the painful division which—as I
hope—may finally also find its fitting peaceful solution in a united Europe.

Allow me, ladies and gentlemen, to stress with particular joy in this place, among the efforts for peace with which your country too tries to contribute in an authoritative way to worldwide understanding among peoples, the growing readiness for agreement between your citizens and the Polish people. In this connection no slight credit goes, as is known, also to evangelical Christians as well as to the bishops and Catholics in both countries. In all painful relations between peoples the following principle holds good: not the reckoning of the grave wrongs and sorrows inflicted upon one another, but only the desire for reconciliation and the common search for new ways of peaceful coexistence can pave the way and guarantee a better future for peoples.

Likewise it does particular credit to your leaders in politics, the Church, and society, that they are increasingly aware of the heavy responsibility incumbent on well-to-do countries with regard to Third World countries, and try to meet it through programs and initiatives of the government and of the Church, as well as through concrete actions of aid on the part of citizens. In this field, too, many praiseworthy achievements have already taken place. However, as I was able to realize personally through my recent apostolic journeys in some of these countries, and as the competent North-South Commission strongly emphasized in its conclusive report, far greater efforts must be made and even more decisive measures taken on the national and international plane to combat more effectively and with more hope of success the hunger and structural misery in underprivileged countries and continents. If development is the new name for peace, as Pope Paul VI stressed in his Encyclical *Popu-*

lorum progressio, an even stronger and more disinterested common commitment for the interests of Third World peoples is the most urgent imperative of the time, in order to guarantee world peace in a lasting way. For this purpose even a considerable self-limitation of the rich nations should not be an unacceptable sacrifice.

REAL PROGRESS
SERVES THE WHOLE MAN

4. The many good and positive things that take place also in the world of today—despite many prophets of disaster, thanks precisely to the new technical achievement, with a range of operation that is all the greater, in order to make the conditions of life of the whole human family and of each individual more worthy of man—inspire in us joy and gratitude to God, who is also the Lord of our time. The Church, by virtue of her mission of salvation, stimulates and supports as much as possible everything that can contribute to elevating and developing the whole man, as is clearly illustrated also by the trusting collaboration and partnership between state and Church in various areas and at various levels in your country.

This recognition of the good and praiseworthy things in modern society must let us recognize at the same time, however, the privations and dangers to which man is more and more exposed today. The brighter the light, the more clearly the shadows and the threatening darkness of mistaken developments are revealed. "A critical analysis of our modern civilization," as I said last year in my address to the United Nations, "shows that in the last hundred years it has contributed as never before to the development of material goods, but that it has also given rise, both in theory and still more in practice, to a series of attitudes in which sensitivity to the spiritual dimension of human existence is diminished to a greater or less extent, as a result of certain premises which reduce the meaning of human life chiefly to the many different material and economic factors—I mean to the demands of production, the market, consumption, the accumulation of riches or of the growing bureaucracy with which an attempt is made to regulate these very processes'' (Address of His Holiness, Pope John Paul II, to the XXXIV General Assembly of the United Nations Organization, October 2, 1979, no. 15).

All presumed progress is real progress only when it serves the whole man. This wholeness of man, in addition to the material values, necessarily includes also spiritual and moral values. Therefore, ''the progress of humanity must be measured not only by the progress of science and technology,...but also and chiefly by the primacy given to spiritual values and by the progress of moral life'' (*ibid.,* no. 7).

So it is a very deplorable error of great consequence, when in modern society legitimate pluralism is often confused with neutrality of values and, in the name of misunderstood democracy, people think they can increasingly do without ethical norms and the use of the moral category of good and evil in public life.

MAN'S LIKENESS TO GOD

5. This development, whose negative effects can be seen even in life within the Church, gives rise to growing attention and concern in her. Since her foundation by Jesus Christ, who solemnly declared before

Pilate and in the imminence of His death, that He had been born and had come into the world to bear witness to truth (cf. Jn. 18:37), the Church, in virtue of her mission, together with the Good News of redemption and salvation as its indispensable premise, has always emphatically recognized, stimulated, and defended precisely the spiritual-moral dimension of the human person. She does so not only out of fidelity to the revealed teaching entrusted to her, but also out of a deep awareness of responsibility for man, for whose service and spiritual welfare she knows she is sent. The Church professes man's likeness to God and, consequently, his inviolable dignity. On it are based, finally, his inalienable fundamental rights as well as the fundamental values for a social life worthy of man. The debate on fundamental values, which has been so heated in your country in the last few years, underlies the particular relevance and necessity of this new reminder of the solid foundations of our modern civilization and society.

In accordance with the prophetic office handed down to her, the Church can never fail, in the name of truth, to point out as a moral transgression or sin everything notoriously in contradiction with man's dignity and God's commandment. In particular, she cannot be silent when such lofty rights as human life, in any form or in any stage whatever, runs the risk of being disposed of.

The Church is sent to bear witness to truth, and thereby she makes a valuable contribution to creating a social and public life worthy of man. In season or out of season, she recalls man's high dignity and vocation as God's creature. This dignity, recognizable for everyone, shines forth in all its clarity and greatness in Jesus Christ, in the message of His life and in His teaching. In Him alone—this is the conviction of Christian faith—man experiences the whole truth about himself. "When all is said and done, man cannot understand himself without Christ," as I stressed in my sermon in Victory Square in Warsaw. "He cannot grasp who he is, nor what his true dignity consists of, nor what his vocation and his final destiny are" (cf. *L'Osservatore Romano*, German Weekly Edition, June 8, 1979, p. 5). If Christians take the truth about man revealed in Christ as the foundation of their witness of life and their social activity, this will be a service for everyone: human dignity, recognizable for everyone and which must be recognized by everyone, stands out all the more clearly and completely.

DEEP MORAL RENEWAL FROM THE ROOTS

6. I would not like to conclude these brief reflections of mine, ladies and gentlemen, without appealing to you, particularly those of you who share with me the same convictions of faith, to become aware again of the Christian foundations of the history of your people and of the constitution of your modern state, which bears the Christian stamp. Deep moral renewal can take place effectively only from within, from the roots. After the great ideologies and messianisms of the last century, apparently so promising, have so wretchedly failed and have driven mankind to the edge of the abyss, today the Church all the more energetically encourages the peoples and all those responsible for them to remember man again, his true dignity and his inalienable fundamental rights—in a

word: man in Christ—in order to construct, starting from Him and together with Him, the present for a better future, in hopeful confidence. Only in this way can the possibility arise, not only for the individual nations but also for Europe and the whole of humanity, of overcoming in a way worthy of man the dangers looming up more and more on the horizon of history, and of a really fulfilled life for all peoples and men in truth, justice and peace.

I, therefore, invoke for you, ladies and gentlemen, and for your whole people, light and strength from God, the principle and end of all history, as well as His abiding protection and blessing.

WITNESS OF FULLEST AND DEEPEST FAITH

With a solemn Eucharistic concelebration presided over by the Holy Father on Sunday morning, November 16, in the "Illos Höhe" stadium in Osnabrück, the second day of the Pope's apostolic pilgrimage in the Federal Republic of Germany began. During the Liturgy of the Word the Holy Father delivered the following homily.

Venerable confrères,
Dear brothers and sisters in the Lord!

1. When John the Evangelist, on the basis of his familiar relations with his Master and deep knowledge of Christ's loving heart, drew up the words of today's Gospel, the Lord's farewell prayer, he had in mind the first Christian communities: they had been formed only with difficulty and slowly, first in Palestine, then, after the first persecution and flight, in Antioch, and from there, under St. Paul's missionary impetus, in Asia Minor, Greece, and even in Rome. These communities lived as a minority amid the vast majority of pagans in the Roman Empire.

The evangelist wishes to comfort and strengthen these Christians by writing to them how Jesus Christ Himself prayed precisely for them: to them Jesus manifested the "Name" of God; to them He gave His "Glory"; in them must remain the "Love" which exists between God the Father and the Son; they must "become perfectly one," as Jesus is with the Father. Powerful words of comfort and inner strengthening for a life of toil in "dispersion," in the "diaspora"!

My brothers and sisters! Today I bring to all of you this Gospel, this joyful message, this efficacious prayer of Jesus: it is valid for you, faithful of this ancient and venerable diocese, which has just celebrated the twelfth centenary of its foundation; and it is valid for all Catholics in the diaspora in north Germany and in Scandinavia, whom I would like to address in particular today from this city of Osnabrück, the See of the northernmost diocese of the country.

I greet with particular joy the bishops present here from this diocese and neighboring ones, especially Berlin and Scandinavia, and also the priests and faithful of those diaspora regions and countries. The Supreme Pastor of the Church, which lives united among many peoples, has come to you to thank God together with you for the courage of your faith, and also to strengthen you in it so that you will continue to be living witnesses of our redemption in Christ.

DIFFICULT SITUATION

2. In this very vast diaspora, the situation of Christians as regards faith is very varied and difficult. Moreover, in the dioceses of north Germany, it is also decisively characterized by a particular historical circumstance. At the end of the war, hundreds of thousands of persons, including many Catholics who had to leave their native land, flocked into large areas of these dioceses and settled there among a population which until then had been almost exclusively

evangelical. Together with their few worldly possessions, these people brought with them the precious
treasure of their faith, which was often symbolized
only in the well-worn prayer book of their former
homeland.

Many of you, dear brothers and sisters in faith,
still remember how you had to seek a new home in a
foreign land then, and strive to provide for the most
basic needs, and how hundreds of new Catholic communities had to be founded at the same time. Under
the guidance of energetic bishops and priests, you
built new churches and erected new altars. Although
you yourselves lived in want and were deeply concerned about your families, you set to work at once,
in your new country, to build up ecclesial life, and
made many sacrifices in order to do so. In this way
you bore witness before the whole world that you remained staunch in faith, that you did not let yourselves become bitter because of the cross laid upon
you, and were even able to change sorrow into blessing, and discord into reconciliation. We must be very
grateful to you all for this example of constancy in
faith.

Looking back at the development of ecclesial life
in those difficult years, let us also remember with
gratitude the many evangelical communities in this
country, which for a long time put their churches also
at the disposal of Catholics, thus enabling their pastors to gather again the dispersed flock.

A RESPONSIBLE FAITH

3. Hard times did, in fact, inflict bitter wounds;
but the Lord also healed and helped. It seems ap-

propriate to remember this on this very day, when your country commemorates with a "day of national mourning" the countless victims of the last war. But the same Lord Jesus Christ, who assisted you yesterday with His consoling support, will also confer on you today and tomorrow the power of His love, so that, amid the trials of the present time, we may remain credible witnesses to His message of freedom.

So—according to the words of the Second Reading of today's liturgical celebration, taken from the First Letter of Peter—you have even good reasons to "rejoice, though now for a little while you may have to suffer various trials, so that the genuineness of your faith, more precious than gold which though perishable, is tested by fire..." (1 Pt. 1:6-7). The test of your faith: that is your chance! A deep, mature and responsible faith: this can be your gift to the whole Church! And so you yourselves can, "as the outcome of your faith,...obtain the salvation of your souls" (v. 9), which will be granted to you "at the revelation of Jesus Christ." "Without having seen him, you love him; though you do not now see him, you believe in him" (v. 8). Through His resurrection from the dead you have "a living hope" to an "inheritance which is imperishable, undefiled, and unfading, kept in heaven for you" (vv. 3-4). It is "God's power" itself that strengthens you in this faith (v. 5), if—we may add—you do everything possible to keep your faith alive and strong. Your situation as Christians in the diaspora is a particular challenge to do so.

Very few of us can still let ourselves be carried along today in the practice of faith simply by an environment of deep faith. We must rather decide consciously to want to be practicing Christians, and to have the courage to distinguish ourselves, if necessary, from our environment. The premise for such a decided testimony of Christian life is to perceive and grasp faith as a precious chance of life, which transcends the interpretations and praxis of the environment. We must take advantage of every opportunity to experience how faith enriches our existence, cultivates an authentic faith in us in the battle of life, strengthens our hope against the attacks of all forms of pessimism and despair, urges us to avoid all extremism and to commit ourselves after reflection to justice and peace in the world; finally, it can console us and relieve us in sorrow. The task and the chance of the diaspora situation is, therefore, to experience in a more conscious way how faith helps us to live in a fuller and deeper way.

CALLED TO COMMUNITY

4. But no one believes only for himself. The Lord called His disciples to be a community, the pilgrim People of God, the Church, in which His vital power circulates as in a living body. Where several faithful meet for a common profession of faith, celebration, prayer and action, the Lord comes to meet them. "For where two or three are gathered in my name, there am I in the midst of them" (Mt. 18:20). As if the Lord already wished with these words to refer to a diaspora situation, He does not speak of a thousand, or of a hundred, or of ten, but of "two or three." Even in this case the Lord promises us His strengthening presence!

Your dioceses and parish communities offer various possibilities of meeting not only with one or two fellow Christians in faith, but with entire communities and groups. I would like here to thank heartily all priests and lay assistants who, in spite of great difficulties, tirelessly commit themselves with zeal and abnegation for an active and fruitful community life. At the same time I invite all believers to use all the opportunities that arise for the greater good of their faith and their future in God. Be particularly faithful and constant in taking part in holy Mass on Sundays or on Saturday evenings. And where it is impossible to reach the Sunday Eucharistic celebration due to great distances, but where there is a Liturgy of the Word—perhaps with the distribution of Holy Communion—take part in it! Where we are gathered in the name of Jesus, He is present in our midst.

EVANGELICAL BRETHREN

5. But I would like above all to encourage you to seek and deepen, in sincere faith, contact with your evangelical brethren. The ecumenical movement in the last few decades has clearly shown you how much evangelical Christians are united with you in their concerns and joys, and how much you have in common with them when you live faith in our Lord Jesus Christ together, sincerely and consistently. So let us thank God from the bottom of our hearts that the various ecclesial communities in your regions are no longer divided by misunderstanding or even barricaded against one another in fear. You rather have already had the happy experience that mutual understanding and acceptance were particularly easy when both sides knew their own faith well, professed it

joyfully, and encouraged concrete communion with their own brothers in faith. I would like to encourage you to continue along this way.

Live your Faith as Catholics with gratitude to God and to your ecclesial community; bear a credible witness, in all humility and without any complacency, to the deep values of your Faith; and encourage, discreetly and amiably, also your evangelical brothers to strengthen and deepen in Christ their own convictions and forms of religious life. If all Churches and communities really grow in the fullness of the Lord, His Spirit will certainly indicate to us the way to reach full internal and external unity of the Church.

Jesus Himself prayed for the perfect unity of His followers: "That they may all be one; even as you, Father, are in me, and I in you, that they also may be one in us, so that the world may believe that you have sent me" (Jn. 17:21). We have just heard it in the Gospel. And once more, even more earnestly, Jesus prays to His divine Father: "The glory which you have given me I have given to them, that they may be one even as we are one, I in them and you in me, that they may become perfectly one, so that the world may know that you have sent me and have loved them even as you have loved me" (Jn. 17:22-23).

PRAYER FOR UNITY

This prayer for unity, precisely by Christ's will, must apply also to all those Christians who support and strengthen one another in faith: "I do not pray for these only, but also for those who believe in me through their word" (v. 20). We can confidently hope, therefore, that all ecumenical dialogues, all prayers and common actions of Christians of different denominations, are already included in this fervent prayer of Jesus: "That they may all be one; even as you, Father, are in me, and I in you, that they may also be one in us." The credibility of the message of redemption through the death and resurrection of Christ depends on this unity: "so that the world may believe that you have sent me" (v. 21). In the same prayer, the Lord sets one condition: "I made known to them your name, and I will make it known, that the love with which you have loved me may be in them, and I in them" (v. 26). We will pray and act in a really ecumenical way "in the name of Jesus" only when we keep love of Christ among us and put it at the basis of all efforts for deeper unity.

I am firmly confident that this prayer of the Son of God, our Lord and Brother, for the unity of all Christians, will yield its full fruit one day. We wish to ask Him to let what the prophet announced in today's First Reading become a reality in us: "I will take you from the nations, and gather you from all the countries, and bring you into your own land. I will sprinkle clean water upon you, and you shall be clean.... A new heart I will give you, and a new spirit I will put within you.... And I will put my spirit within you and cause you to walk in my statutes and be careful to observe my ordinances...and you shall be my people, and I will be your God" (Ez. 26:24-28).

NEVER-FAILING SPRING

6. Dear brothers and sisters! You are certainly living your faith under difficult conditions. Other

dioceses of your country, better situated, are, however, close to you in solidarity with various forms of aid, especially through the well-deserving and tested institution, the Work of St. Boniface. You, in your turn, take part in the Work of St. Anskar, with which you support and assist the dioceses of Scandinavia in a brotherly way. In the kingdom of God, he who knows how to share does not lose anything; on the contrary, he then becomes a real disciple of Christ, who became poor for us, to make us all rich (cf. 2 Cor. 8:9).

The existence of the Christian in the diaspora must be sustained by awareness of belonging to a great community of men, to the People of God gathered from all the peoples of this earth. Even in "dispersion" you are, together with your priests and bishops, united in various ways with the Church of your whole country and with the universal Church. Therefore, I consider it a very happy occasion to be able, as Bishop of Rome, to be in your midst today, on the second day of my visit in Germany, precisely in this episcopal see with its connections in the extreme north of Europe, in order to celebrate the holy Eucharist with you.

The Eucharist means the thanksgiving of the believing community to the Lord "in communion with the whole Church," as we pray in the First Eucharistic Prayer of Mass. Today, together with all believers in God, we wish to thank Him particularly for all the gifts with which He confirmed and strengthened your faith and your love for the Church, even in difficult circumstances and hard times. The celebration of the Mass is itself a never-failing spring

*As believers, in fact, you are never "few,"
never "alone," but always united with "the
many" who follow Christ with you throughout
the wide world, in faith and hope, and bear
witness to His redeeming love. He is the power
of our faith and the foundation of our trust.
May He bless you and your families and guide
your pilgrimage as Catholics up to its eternal
goal, the definitive gathering of all believers
from the dispersion of this world to His eternal
kingdom. Amen.*

of strength for religious life and the preservation of every Christian in faith. It keeps and nourishes our communion with Christ through living communion with His Mystical Body, the Church.

COMMUNION OF BELIEVERS

Likewise, when the Lord's bread is broken and His body offered in Holy Communion, we live and realize in a clear and perceptible way this deep unity of the body of Christ, the communion of all believers. Gain a new awareness today, in joyful gratitude, of this deep and intimate union of the whole Church beyond all human boundaries and barriers! Take away this awareness as a precious treasure to your communities, to your neighborhood, to your families! As believers, in fact, you are never "few," never "alone," but always united with "the many" who follow Christ with you throughout the wide world, in faith and hope, and bear witness to His redeeming love. He is the power of our faith and the foundation of our trust. May He bless you and your families and guide your pilgrimage as Catholics up to its eternal goal, the definitive gathering of all believers from the dispersion of this world to His eternal kingdom. Amen.

DEEPENING THE SPIRIT OF BROTHERHOOD

After the Mass celebrated at Osnabrück on November 16, the Holy Father met representatives of the ecclesial organizations engaged in welfare work. The Pope delivered the following address.

Dear brothers and sisters!

As I stressed yesterday on my arrival in your country, my pastoral visit is intended to be also an expression of recognition and gratitude to the bishops, priests, and laity of your Church, who beyond the borders attend so generously to the needs of brothers and sisters in underprivileged areas.

My sincere thanks are addressed, therefore, also to you who represent the various works and institutions created and constantly supported by German bishops, religious, and laity for service of the Church in the world: "Misereor," "Adveniat," "Missio," German Caritas and the Work of St. Boniface, to mention only the most important ones. I thank you also for the contribution of German Catholics to the "European Solidarity Fund" and to "Aid for Priests in the East."

The universal Church is realized in the local churches in communion with one another. The works and institutions you represent have contributed a great deal to deepening the spirit of brotherhood among men. Keep, dear brothers and sisters, and always promote among believers, this readiness to help others and these sentiments of universality. They spring from a brotherly and good heart to which the Lord gives the joy of sharing bread with the poor and faith in Christ with all peoples on earth. May Christ the Lord strengthen you in this with my special apostolic blessing.

ACCEPT SORROW TRUSTFULLY: THE LORD COMES ALONG THIS WAY

The Holy Father recited the Marian prayer "Angelus Domini" in Osnabrück Cathedral shortly after 12:30 on Sunday, November 16. Before the prayer, the Holy Father, addressing the many handicapped present, delivered the following address.

Dear brothers and sisters,

It is a great joy for me to be able to address you right at the beginning with this beautiful name: brothers and sisters. For we are all children of the one common Father, loved and redeemed by God in Christ. So we are not strangers, unknown to one another, even if we meet here for the first time. I heartily greet all of you who are gathered in this cathedral, to recite together with me the ancient and familiar prayer of the "Angelus Domini."

Our communion in prayer at noon today includes not only you here, but many other brothers and sisters all over Germany who have to bear the burden of some handicap in their life, and who wish to join in faith in our midday prayer with the help of television and the radio. I would like to call you, too, my brothers and sisters, who at home—alone or with members of your family and friends—or in the larger community of an institute, are joined with us here in Osnabrück through the media. Together with you all, we are about to praise God and thank Him for the great gift of His love.

This love is the foundation of your hope and courage in life. God showed us in Jesus Christ in an unsurpassable way how He loves every person and thereby confers infinite dignity on him. Precisely those who suffer handicaps in body or in spirit can know they are friends of Jesus, specially loved by Him. He Himself says: "Come to me, all who labor and are heavy-laden, and I will give you rest. Take my yoke upon you, and learn from me; for I am gentle and lowly in heart, and you will find rest for your souls. For my yoke is easy, and my burden is light" (Mt. 11:28-30). What seems to men weakness and frailty, is for God a reason for special love and assistance. This judgment of God is then a mandate and obligation also for the Church and for every individual Christian. For us Christians it is less important whether one is sick or healthy; what finally counts is this: Are you ready to realize as a real Christian, with awareness and faith, the dignity conferred on you by God, in all the situations of your life and in your behavior—or do you want to lose this dignity of yours in a superficial and irresponsible life, in sin and guilt before God? Even as handicapped you can become saints, you can all reach the high goal that God has assigned to every person as His beloved creature.

Every man receives from God his own personal vocation, his particular mandate of salvation. Whatever form God's will for us assumes, it is, when all is said and done, always a joyful message for us, a message for our eternal salvation. This also holds true for you who are called as badly handicapped persons to a quite particular way of following Him, the way of the cross. With the above-mentioned words Christ calls upon you to take your sorrows as His yoke, as a way of following in His footsteps. Only in this way will you not collapse under the weight of painful burdens. The only proper answer to God's call to follow Christ, whatever concrete form it may assume, is the answer of the Blessed Virgin: "Let it be done to me according to your word" (Lk. 1:38). Only your prompt "yes" to God's will, which is often beyond our human comprehension, can make you blessed and bestow on you, even now, a deep joy that cannot be destroyed from outside by any necessity.

For this purpose you need, of course, the active help of many healthy fellow men. I am thinking especially of you who have come here as helpers or attendants or, wherever you may be, assist the handicapped, constantly ready to help them. As relatives or for professional reasons, you put your skills, your time, and your energies in the service of your neighbor. In the name of Jesus Christ, who meets you mysteriously in your suffering brothers and sisters themselves, I would like to thank you for this self-sacrificing service and at the same time encourage you in it. The Lord's promising words go to such disinterested servants: "Come, O blessed of my Father.... I was sick and you visited me," handicapped and you assisted me. "Inherit the kingdom prepared for you from the foundation of the world" (Mt. 25:34-35).

I address an equally cordial word of thanks and encouragement also to all the priests who, as chaplains of the handicapped, carry out an important role in the Church. You are in a particular way servants of your deep spiritual joy. Do not tire, in spite of the pressing shortage of clergy, to bring the glad news to the handicapped with priestly zeal and expert ability. Help them to consider their fate in the light of faith, which teaches them to understand it as a call to share in Christ's redeeming sufferings. Be strong in Christ, who sends you, and through you carries out His work of salvation among men.

Finally, all men and the whole of society are called to assist and help the handicapped. They are entitled to this help. There can be no dividing barriers and walls between healthy persons and them. He who seems to be healthy today, may already bear a disease concealed within him; tomorrow he may have an accident and remain permanently injured. We are all pilgrims along a stretch of road that is very limited, and one day the way will end for each of us with death. Already in times when we are well, most of us feel signs of limitation and weakness, of failing strength and impediment. So let us stand side by side, the more or less healthy, and the more or less handicapped, in brotherly solidarity, and render one another the due brotherly service, through which alone a worthy human common life can be effectively promoted, in the family and in society.

So at this meeting with our handicapped brothers and sisters, all those, here or outside in the country, who are listening to us and watching us, are sincerely invited to join in our midday prayer. Before God all earthly distinctions vanish. There remains decisively only the respective measure of faith, hope, and disinterested love, which each one bears in his heart.

In the prayer of the "Angelus Domini" with the usual three "Ave Maria's," we meditate on the central mystery of our Faith, the Incarnation of God in the womb of the Virgin Mary. As Mary said "yes" to this plan of salvation of God, so we too profess our "fiat," our "yes," to our vocation. Let us trustfully say "yes" to the call to suffering as well as to that of assistance and service! And just as from the Virgin Mary the Word of God became flesh and our Brother, so our way, too, will become fruitful with the power of God. Pain accepted trustfully, service rendered out of love: this is a way today, through which the Lord wishes to come into the world.

So let us fold our hands and recite the Angelus: "The Angel of the Lord...."

SIGNIFICANCE OF WORK IN REDEMPTION

On Sunday, November 16, during the Mass celebrated at the Finthen Air Base in Mainz for the representatives of the millions of workers in the Federal Republic of Germany, the Holy Father delivered the following homily.

Dear brothers and sisters,

1. "Grace to you and peace from God our Father and the Lord Jesus Christ" (Phil. 1:2). With this blessing of the Apostle I greet you all from the bottom of my heart. My brotherly greeting goes to the venerated Bishop of the Diocese of Mainz, Cardinal Hermann Volk, and to the bishops and priests present: in particular, however, it goes today to you, dear Catholic men and women workers from near and far.

The liturgy of this Sunday, the Word of God which we have listened to in deep meditation, prepares us particularly to deal with those important subjects suggested by your presence and by the words of greeting addressed to me at the beginning.

The meeting with the world of work, which has been made possible for me at Mainz, near the tomb of a great precursor and apostle of the social question of last century, namely, Bishop Wilhelm Emmanuel von Ketteler of Mainz, brings to my mind vivid memories of a whole series of similar meetings in the period of my service in St. Peter's See (Guadalajara and Monterrey in Mexico; the meeting at Jasna Gora in Poland with the great mass of miners and steel workers from Silesia; Limerick in Ireland; Des Moines in the United States; Turin, the largest industrial city in Italy; St. Denis in the suburbs of Paris; and finally São Paolo in Brazil). They are always meetings that are particularly important not only from the social point of view, but also from that of the Gospel. The problem of human work is placed at the center of the Creator's covenant with man, made in His image and likeness, and which He strengthened and renewed in Jesus Christ, who Himself spent many years in a workshop in Nazareth.

It is not surprising, therefore, that the social question, bound to the reality of human work as its foundation, should take a central place in the declarations of the ecclesiastical Magisterium. It undeniably belongs to the proclamation of the Gospel, especially in the present world.

If we therefore take up today's subject, we want to follow the voice of the liturgy, which sets us "before the Lord, for he comes, / for he comes to judge the earth. / He will judge the world with righteousness, / and the peoples with his truth" (Ps. 95 [96]:13).

The shape of human justice and the measure that must be applied to the whole social question, which is still in expansion, must be seen from the definitive perspective of the justice of God Himself. The liturgy of this Sunday, next to last in the liturgical year, is of great help to us.

APOSTOLATE OF WORK

2. In the reading of the Second Letter of St. Paul to the Thessalonians, the subject of human work is dealt with in a completely open and direct way on the basis of the Apostle's personal experience: "We were not idle when we were with you, we did not eat anyone's bread without paying, but with toil and labor we worked night and day, that we might not burden any of you. It was not because we have not that right, but to give you in our conduct an example to imitate" (2 Thes. 3:7-9).

Paul of Tarsus combined his mission and his apostolic service with work, with work as an artisan. Just as Christ combined His work of redemption with work in the workshop at Nazareth, so Paul combined the apostolate with the work of his hands. May that be a reminder for many of you, in fact for all, a reminder to the whole Christian world of work: look at the question of work in the dimensions of the work of redemption and combine work with the apostolate! The Church of our time particularly needs this apostolate of work: the apostolate of the workers and the apostolate among the workers, in order to illuminate this wide area of life with the light of the Gospel. Just as Bishop Ketteler did! The light of truth and of God's love must shine forth upon man's work! It must not be dominated by the shadows of injustice, exploitation, hatred and man's humiliation!

In this apostolate a great task falls upon the apostolate of workers in dioceses and communities as well as on the efficiency of your associations, which are dedicated mainly to the world of work. Obviously workers feel more than others the harmful effect of

Just as Christ combined His work of redemption with work in the workshop at Nazareth, so Paul combined the apostolate with the work of his hands. May that be a reminder for many of you, in fact for all, a reminder to the whole Christian world of work: look at the question of work in the dimensions of the work of redemption and combine work with the apostolate!

deep alienation, with all its repercussions on faith. I wish to call to new and more energetic efforts your associations in particular, which have already won many historical merits, especially the Catholic Workers' Movement, Young Christian Workers, and Kolping's Work—for love of men created by God and redeemed by Christ.

CATHOLIC SOCIAL DOCTRINE

3. In the Second Letter to the Thessalonians, we read: "Now such persons we command and exhort in the Lord Jesus Christ to do their work in quietness and to earn their own living" (3:12). Just before, the Apostle expressed the same thought in a very graphic way: "If any one will not work, let him not eat" (*ibid.*, 3:10).

These clear words, read in the context of the present development of the social question, lead us to recall the principles of Catholic social doctrine. They were set forth, in the encyclical *Rerum novarum* issued by my venerated Predecessor Leo XIII in the year 1891, in innumerable declarations of the ecclesiastical Magisterium, and especially of the Second Vatican Council, with deeply felt pastoral care; they were explained in numerous works by many Catholic scholars, especially German-speaking ones, and communicated to the Christian working people by the multiple effort of zealous pastors of souls and responsible lay people. Do not let this spiritual inheritance of precursors in the field of the social question wither miserably, but, on the contrary, let it bear concrete fruit for the old and new problems with which you are concerned.

At the center of all reflections on the world of work and the economy, there must always be man. With all the objective justice required, respect for the inviolable dignity of man must always be decisive, and not just of the individual worker, but also of his family; not just the men of today, but also those of future generations.

From this principle which demands, even more than in the past, a change of thought, light also falls on understanding of the problems in your country, which I càn recall only briefly here, but which are clearly present in my mind.

I am thinking, for example, of those whose job is in danger or those who have already lost it. After very careful examination, a restructuring of groups may turn out to be necessary, and the more honestly this is recognized, the better. But workers who have given the best of themselves for many years must never be the only ones to bear the disadvantages! Be united in solidarity with them and help them to find another meaningful activity. You have already given encouraging examples!

I am thinking of the workers you have called from other countries and who, together with you, have created what you are enjoying today. In the problems that have arisen, your sense of responsibility will find solutions that do not offend their human sensibility and will meet the spiritual good of their families.

Further and even deeper problems are derived from our coming up against the limits of economic growth more and more frequently. Even if we do not wish it, we are obliged by development to abandon our claims and renounce something, in order to share the limited goods peacefully with the largest number of men possible. If the social climate begins to stiffen, the subsequent processes of change can be overcome only by objective discussion and in the united collaboration of everyone.

WORLDWIDE DIMENSION

4. In consideration of these important problems concerning justice and widespread social welfare, we can never confine ourselves within the boundaries of a country, a community of countries, or even a continent. Today the social question has a worldwide human dimension. This emerges clearly from the declarations of the Magisterium of the last Popes *(Mater et magistra, Populorum progressio)* and of the Second Vatican Council. It is often said that from this point of view there is a tension between the West and the East, but the tension between the North and the South is no less significant. By "North" is meant the area of the rich countries, which live in a certain abundance. The "South," especially the so-called Third World, designates that area of countries whose populations are often underdeveloped from the economic point of view, lead a life of hardships, and are even exposed to hunger and starvation.

As citizens, you have the duty to create a political climate which will enable the State, especially the rich ones, to give effective aid for development in all the necessary forms to those underprivileged and not infrequently exploited countries.

As Catholics you started many years ago in your great social institutions to perceive your worldwide co-responsibility in an exemplary way and to an increasing extent. Do not desist from your efforts! Open your heart even more deeply to the necessities of those countries, sometimes desperate ones! As Supreme Pastor of the Church, on whose shoulders there weighs an immediate responsibility for those countries as well, I wish on this occasion to thank you heartily, also on behalf of those poor and extremely poor people, for your efforts and sacrifices. In particular I thank all believers of your country for the latest sign of cordial solidarity, namely for the collection made on the occasion of my pastoral visit to relieve the extremely distressing situation in the Sahel region in Central Africa.

This world dimension of the social question is an appeal to our human and Christian conscience; it will mark the last quarter of this century more and more. The search for solutions by all men of good will and the apostolate of all Christians must grow to an ever greater extent in this world dimension. In the name of the Gospel! And at the same time in the name of human solidarity!

JUSTICE AND PEACE

5. The social problem in its present historical dimension, for every people and for the whole of mankind, is closely linked with the central task of guaranteeing peace in the world. *Justitia et pax.* Justice and peace! How the one depends on the other here was shown to us by Pope John XXIII in his encyclical *Pacem in terris.* We must think of it again today, when the liturgy recalls to us Christ's words on "wars and revolutions": "Nation will rise against na-

tion, and kingdom against kingdom; there will be great earthquakes, and in various places famines and pestilences; and there will be terrors and great signs from heaven" (Lk. 21:10ff.).

These words come from the "eschatological" discourse according to Luke. Christ enumerates the various *signs* for the "disappearance of the world in pain"; they are repeated continually in history. For this reason He adds: "When you hear of wars and tumults, do not be terrified; for this must first take place, but the end will not be at once" (Lk. 21:9).

Let us again remember clearly the horrible atrocities of the Second World War, we especially, sons and daughters of European peoples. Let us remember that time of tremendous destruction and indescribable suffering, of outrage and contempt of man. That must never be repeated for the generations of our children and grandchildren, never again among men, either in our continent or elsewhere.

We wish to pray to God incessantly that this dreadful lesson of history may instill in the whole world respect for the rights of every individual man and of every single people. How important that is in our old continent! Concern for peace must never be lacking in the carrying out of our Christian mandate; it can never be lacking in the efforts of all men of good will, especially those who have particular responsibilities here.

We hope that concern for peace will move all those in positions of responsibility to seek a permanent dialogue on the different problems—however serious and complex they may be—and thus strengthen longed-for peace from day to day. How could we not desire at the same time that the Madrid meeting, on security and collaboration in Europe, may also contribute to strengthening peace in full respect of the rights of every individual man and every people, including religious freedom, on the basis of the principles recognized in the conclusive Helsinki Document.

May the efficient application of this authoritative principle of human rights and of the rights of individual peoples banish from the life of humanity all forms of imperialism, aggression, dominion, exploitation, and colonialism!

I say this also as the son of a nation which, in the course of the centuries, has greatly suffered and has been obliged to defend these rights of man and of the people with great determination.

And now hear the cry of blessing of today's liturgy, with the words of the prophet Malachi: may "the sun of righteousness" rise, and its rays bring salvation (cf. 4:2) for everyone.

PRAY FOR ALL PEOPLE

6. In today's Gospel Christ also says: "Take heed that you are not led astray; for many will come in my name, saying, 'I am he!' and, 'The time is at hand!' Do not go after them" (Lk. 21:8).

Dear brothers and sisters! We beg you: remain firm, unshakable in the truth of the Gospel! Go in its light along the paths of justice and peace! No one must lead us astray!

Christ says further: "They will lay their hands on you and persecute you, delivering you up to the synagogues and prisons, and you will be brought before kings and governors for my name's sake'' (Lk. 21:12).

Dear brothers and sisters! Let us pray for all the people in the world! Let us pray particularly for our brothers and sisters in faith, whose rights are being violated. Let us pray for those who are suffering because of repressions, who are denied what derives from the principle of freedom of conscience and religion, wherever it may be in the wide world....

Christ says finally: "Settle it beforehand in your minds, not to meditate beforehand how to answer; for I will give you a mouth and wisdom, which none of your adversaries will be able to withstand or contradict. You will be delivered up even by parents and brothers and kinsmen and friends, and some of you they will put to death; you will be hated by all for my name's sake. But not a hair of your head will perish. By your endurance you will gain your lives" (Lk. 21:14-19).

Dear brothers and sisters! We are thinking of all those, also your fellow-countrymen, who have been faithful to this word of our Redeemer and Master in a heroic way! Let us pray that we may all remain faithful! Let us pray to the Lord to give us always His spirit of strength. especially in hours and times of trial! And that we may bear witness to Him day after day.

APOSTLE OF THE GOSPEL

7. Christ says: "This will be a time for you to bear testimony" (Lk. 21:13). Let us thank Him for these words. Let us thank Him for this extraordinary opportunity to be able to bear witness to a Gospel of peace

and justice, here in Mainz, near the tomb of the great pioneer and apostle of this Gospel, Bishop Wilhelm Emmanuel von Ketteler.

For all of you, who honor the name of the Lord, may the sun of justice rise for ever, and may salvation come to you with its rays. Amen.

On this happy occasion I wish to extend a word of greeting and gratitude to the members of the American community present here today. Your collaboration in preparing for this gathering is deeply appreciated. I pray that the Spirit of God will give you in abundance the justice, peace and joy that constitute the kingdom of God. And on our part, dear brothers and sisters, let us all, in the words of St. Paul, "make it our aim to work for peace and to strengthen one another" (Rom. 14:19). And may the love of God abide always in your hearts.

DEFEND YOUR FAITH WITH YOUR CULTURAL IDENTITY

The last meeting of the second day of the Pope's apostolic pilgrimage took place on Sunday, November 16, in front of Mainz Cathedral, where representatives of the Polish community residing in the territory of the Federal Republic were gathered. The Holy Father delivered the following address.

Dear fellow-countrymen,
Beloved brothers and sisters,

1. I thank divine Providence and man because I am able, during this pilgrimage of mine on German soil, to meet my fellow-countrymen, on whom it has fallen, here in Germany, to live and work, create their history, that of their families, their country, and, at the same time, the history of salvation. This history of Christ's ways to man and of man's ways to God is decisive for man and only in it can man fully find himself again, read again the value and the capabilities of his heart, and find a rightful place in the world.

It is precisely these divine ways of salvation, grace, power, and love that we wish to find again and again, in the course of this pilgrimage, together with the Church in Germany, with its pastors and its faithful, with our brothers and sisters in faith in Christ, and also with all men of good will.

HISTORICAL CATHEDRAL

2. Gathered before the millenary Cathedral of Mainz, which, in the course of whole centuries, was the scene of the coronations of emperors and kings, our thoughts cannot but go to the whole historical process of the formation of the society of peoples in Christian Europe; especially when, on the horizon of history, new nations, new countries were being born to an independent existence, and sometimes at great cost won their place in Europe, in the world, and in history.

We know this process, its lights and shadows, and we know that it was not and is not easy. We know that geographic proximity, neighborhood, must and can be a blessing, but, like everything human, they can also be a curse. If this is so, that means that it is above all a task, a task set before individuals, as well as before whole nations. It was already understood in this way by the second historical sovereign of Poland, King Boleslaw Chrobry, who, through the alliance with Emperor Otto III, brought Poland into the Latin Christian society of Europe as a member with full rights.

HOW THE SAINTS BUILD

3. Only holy men are able to build stable bridges between the nations, because only the saints base their activity on love; on love of man, because they

construct their lives and the future on God. "Love is of God, and he who loves is born of God and knows God...for God is love" (1 Jn. 4:7-8). Only what is built on God, on love, is lasting, as the veneration of Trzebnica, of the tomb of St. Edwige, the patroness of reconciliation—which still goes on now—bears witness.

If the place of believers and saints is occupied by godless men, then selfishness and hatred become the law as is shown by the subsequent history of coexistence between the German and Polish nations.

MANY POLES IN GERMANY

4. In the course of history, amid the successive events, amid political decisions, hatred or friendship, in the midst of all that, there are concrete men who wish to live, develop and maintain their own identity, rights, freedom, faith, and dignity: it is to them above all that my thought goes during this meeting.

In the past century many Poles came to Germany for economic reasons. With hard and tiring work, they contributed to the economic development of the country, which offered them work and bread.

After the First World War, when Poland regained independence, many of them remained in this place. And in the border lands there remained a large number of Poles who had been living there before. They formed a Polish cultural federation for the purpose of cultivating Christian and Polish tradition and culture. These organizations were nearly always led by priests, concerned about harmonious coexistence and the Christian bond of love.

It was not an easy life. You yourselves, perhaps, or your fathers, have been exposed to many humiliations and have suffered because of your religious spirit or your patriotic attitude.

BUILDING ANEW

5. The events of the last World War had a great impact on the society of nations. They brought so many sufferings, damage, and misfortunes.

As a result of these events, after the conclusion of the war nearly two million Poles found themselves on German territory. Some had passed through the Gehenna of the concentration camps; others were exhausted by overwork; others again, brought here by war events, were unable, for various reasons, to return to their homeland. They did not give in to despair. In spite of ordeals and adventures, in spite of the serious material situation due to the destruction of war, they organized themselves at once.

It is a great credit to the Polish priests. Wasting away in the camps, they set to work to organize the religious life of their fellow-countrymen. After the terrible vicissitudes of war, it was again necessary to rebuild faith; faith in God and faith in man. It was again necessary to rebuild trust in man; faith in one's own human dignity! And it was on the foundation of Christ that all this had to be done, because only on His teaching, on the Christian ethics of love, conversion, and forgiveness could the future and the new interhuman society be constructed. And it is a great credit precisely to those priests, ex-prisoners in the concentration camps, that many people returned to normal life, that many people did not give up in the period, difficult from every standpoint, that followed the war, and found again faith, dignity, and love.

PRESERVING VALUES

6. All of you, regardless of the circumstances and time of your arrival, are writing your history here; you are carrying on your dialogue with God, with man, and with the world here. You want to be first-rate citizens and contribute to the development of the country in which you live. You want to ensure your children and grandchildren a better future. Here each of you imprints and leaves an unrepeatable trace of his existence, his life, his faith, his choices, his decisions. Everyone, therefore, must protect, reread, and develop what is inside him, deep down, what is written in his heart; he must remember the land, the heritage from which he grew, which formed him and constitutes an integral part of his psyche and his personality.

This is the spirit of the message addressed to the world by the bishops of our continent on the occasion of the jubilee year of St. Benedict, the patron saint of Europe. We read there among other things: "Freedom and justice require that men and peoples should have sufficient space for the development of their own specific values. Every people, every ethnic minority has an identity, tradition, and culture of its own. These values are of great importance for human progress and for peace..." (Solemn Declaration of the European Bishops, September 28, 1980).

Also, revealed truth reaches man within the framework of a given culture. There is a great danger, therefore, that the abandonment of the values inherited from one's culture may lead to the loss of faith, in particular when the values of the culture of the new environment do not have that Christian character which distinguishes the native culture.

DEVOTION TO MARY

7. There is yet another danger. We must be careful not to let ourselves be unduly fascinated, attracted by technical civilization with a simultaneous risk for faith, for the capacity of loving, in a word, for everything that is decisive for man, for man's full dimension and his vocation.

To be rooted in tradition, in a culture imbued with religious values, as is Polish culture, will ensure that "the selfish culture and the selfish technology of work will not succeed in reducing man to the role of an instrument of work" (Address at Salvador). It is, after all, what man is, and not how much he has, that determines his value. And if man is ready to lose his dignity, faith, and national consciousness only to have more, this attitude cannot but lead to self-contempt.

On the other hand, the man who is aware of his identity, coming from the faith and Christian culture of his ancestors and fathers, will keep his dignity, find respect from others, and be a first-rate member of the society in which he lives.

8. One of the deepest characteristics of Polish piety is the devotion and cult of Mary, the Mother of God.

Here, too, in Germany, wherever Poles live, they have brought in their hearts love for their Mother and have entrusted their fate to her. That was séen particularly in the period following the Second World War. One of the first pastoral initiatives was the pilgrimages to the Marian sanctuaries in Germany.

You have gone, every year until now, on pilgrimage to Neviges, to Maria Buchen at Altötting, or other places, as, for example, for the feast at Hanover.

In all these sanctuaries, as well as in the churches in which you gather regularly, there are images of Our Lady of Czestochowa. Her image has been seen on nearly all your banners. The Black Madonna of Jasna Gora speaks to you of God's love and reminds you of the land in which your roots are. You pray before her, you entrust your families to her, particularly in this period in which the image of Our Lady of Czestochowa is visiting all the Pastoral Centers of the Poles in Germany. Mary, who at the moment of the annunciation believed in the Word, became the first believer in the New Covenant, the Mother of our faith; and she leads us to the fullest knowledge of the one God in the Trinity of Persons.

REVIEWING THE PAST

9. Finding myself before you here today, I cannot forget that our preceding meeting took place in September 1978. Then we were together with the Primate, who was at the head of the delegation of Polish bishops on the invitation of the German bishops. The central point of the meeting with our fellow-countrymen was the sanctuary of the Mother of God at Navites. All that took place just a few weeks after the election of John Paul I. According to human evaluation, no one could have foreseen that it would shortly fall on me to become his successor in Saint Peter's See in Rome. This circumstance gives a particular significance to that meeting.

But once more I wish to go back a few years. In 1974, at that time also in September, I took part in Frankfurt in the fiftieth anniversary of the priestly ordination of the late Mons. Edward Lubowiecki (Apostolic Protonotary), who was before the war a close collaborator of the great Metropolitan of Krakow, Cardinal Adam Stefan Sapieha. After his release from the concentration camp, he stayed here, first as Vicar General of Archbishop J. Gawlina, and then as Canonical Visitor of the Poles in Germany. That stay has remained linked in my memory with the figure of Cardinal J. Döpfner, who died so prematurely, and who celebrated Holy Mass with me at Dachau.

Recalling the figure of Mons. Lubowiecki, I wish at the same time to express my best wishes for all God's blessings for the present rector of the Polish Catholic Mission, Reverend Stefan Leciejewski, and for all priests and sisters, and I wish all my fellow-countrymen the most cordial *Szczesc Boze*.

I will always be grateful to you for your prayers.

WORDS OF THANKS

I willingly impart the apostolic blessing to you present and to all those who have not been able to come, and your families and your dear ones. I warmly embrace the sick and the old, the lonely, and those who are abandoned and forgotten by others.

My hearty greetings and blessings to the young and to the children.

May the grace of our Lord Jesus Christ, the love of God the Father and the fellowship of the Holy Spirit be with you all.

CALLED TO UNITY
IN DIALOGUE
OF TRUTH AND LOVE

The third day of John Paul II's apostolic pilgrimage in the Federal Republic of Germany began in the morning of Monday, November 17, with the meeting with representatives of the Council of the German Evangelical Church, in the Museum Halls of Mainz Cathedral. The Holy Father delivered the following address.

Mr. President of the Council,
Members of the Council of the Evangelical Church in Germany,
Dear fellow-Christians!

"Grace to you and peace from God our Father and the Lord Jesus Christ!" (Rom. 1:7) With these words of the Apostle of the Gentiles I greet you and all those you represent. I heartily thank all those who have made this meeting possible in the country in which the Reformation began. I owe particular thanks to you, Mr. President of the Council, for your helpful words, which recalled to us the dimension of this hour and even more that of our Christian mission. In awareness of these facts we can hope—as Paul once did—that "we may be mutually encouraged" (Rom. 1:12).

Our being together at this early hour is for me a very deep symbol, so that I would like to speak with the words of an ancient hymn: "The dawn is already rising on the horizon, may he rise in us like the dawn; the Son is entirely in his Father and the Father entirely in the Word" *(Lauds,* Monday of the second week in the annual cycle). Our common desire is that Christ may shine forth in our midst and in this land as the light of life and truth.

ALL NEED CONVERSION

I recall at this moment that in 1510-1511 Martin Luther came to Rome as a pilgrim to the tombs of the Princes of the Apostles, but also as one seeking and questioning. Today I come to you, the spiritual heirs of Martin Luther; I come as a pilgrim. I come to set, with this pilgrimage in a changed world, a sign of union in the central mystery of our faith.

Many things claim our attention at this brotherly meeting of ours, far more than we can express in the short time at our disposal and with our limited strength. Allow me to express right at the beginning of our talk what particularly moves me. I do so in connection with the testimony of the Letter to the Romans, that writing which was absolutely decisive for Martin Luther. "This letter is the real masterpiece of the New Testament and the purest Gospel," he wrote in 1522.

In the school of the Apostle of the Gentiles we can become aware that we all need conversion. There is no Christian life without repentance. "There can be no ecumenism worthy of the name without interior conversion" *(Unitatis redintegratio,* no. 7). "Let us no more pass judgment on one another" (Rom. 14:13).

Let us rather recognize our guilt. "All have sinned" (Rom. 3:23) applies also with regard to the grace of unity. We must see and say this in all earnestness and draw our conclusions from it. The most important thing is to recognize more and more deeply what consequences the Lord draws from human failing. Paul reduces it to the same denominator: "where sin increased, grace abounded all the more" (Rom. 5:20). God does not cease to "have mercy upon all" (Rom. 11:32). He gives His Son, He gives Himself, He gives forgiveness, justification, grace, eternal life. We can recognize all this together.

You know that decades of my life have been marked by the experience of the challenging of Christianity by atheism and non-belief. It appears to me all the more clearly how important is our common profession of Jesus Christ, of His word and work in this world, and how we are driven by the urgency of the hour to overcome the differences that divide us, and bear witness to our growing union.

Jesus Christ is the salvation of us all. He is the only Mediator, "whom God put forward as an expiation by his blood, to be received by faith" (Rom. 3:25). "We have peace with God through our Lord Jesus Christ" (Rom. 5:1) and among ourselves. By virtue of the Holy Spirit we are His brothers, really and essentially sons of God. "If children, then heirs, heirs of God and fellow heirs with Christ" (Rom. 8:17).

Reflecting on *Confessio Augustana*, and through numerous contacts, we have realized anew that we believe and profess all that together. This was testified by the German bishops in their pastoral letter "Thy Kingdom Come" (January 20, 1980). They said to Catholic faithful: "Let us rejoice to discover not only partial consent on some truths, but also agreement on the fundamental and central truths. That lets us hope for unity also in the areas of our faith and our life in which we are still divided up to now."

CALLED TO STRIVE TOGETHER FOR UNITY

All the gratitude for what remains to us in common and unites us, cannot make us blind to what still divides us. We must examine it together as far as possible, not to widen the gaps, but to bridge them. We cannot stop at the acknowledgement: "We are and remain divided for ever and against each other." We are called to strive together, in the dialogue of truth and love, to full unity in faith. Only full unity gives us the possibility of gathering with the same sentiments and the same faith at the Lord's one table. We can let the lectures given by Luther on the Letter to the Romans in the years 1516-1517 tell us what this effort above all consists of. He teaches that "faith in Christ through which we are justified, is not just belief in Christ, or more exactly in the person of Christ, but belief in what is Christ's." "We must believe in Him and in what is His." To the question: "What is this, then?", Luther refers to the Church and to her authentic teaching. If the difficulties that exist between us were only a question of "ecclesiastical structures set up by men" (cf. *Confessio Augustana,* VIII), we could and should eliminate them immediately. According to the conviction of Catholics, disagreement revolves around "what is Christ's," around "what is His": His Church and her mission, her message, her sacraments, and the ministries placed in the service of the Word and the Sacrament. The dialogue established since the Council has brought us a good way further in this respect. Precisely in Germany many important steps have been taken. That can inspire us with confidence with regard to problems not yet solved.

TO BEAR WITNESS TOGETHER TO THE TRUTH

We must remain in dialogue and in contact. The questions to be faced together demand by their nature a more comprehensive treatment than is possible here and today. I hope that we will find together the way to continue our dialogue. Certainly the German bishops and the collaborators of the Secretariat for the Union of Christians will give their help in this matter.

We must leave no stone unturned. We must do what unites. We owe it to God and to the world. "Let us then pursue what makes for peace and for mutual upbuilding" (Rom. 14:19). Each of us must say to himself with St. Paul: "Woe to me if I do not preach the Gospel" (1 Cor. 9:16). We are called to be witnesses of the Gospel, witnesses of Christ. His message requires us to bear witness together. Allow me to repeat what I said on June 25 of this year on the occasion of the jubilee of *Confessio Augustana:* "The will of Christ and the signs of the times urge us to common witness in growing fullness of truth and love."

The tasks that await us are great and difficult. If we could count only on our own strength, we would despair. "Likewise the Spirit helps us in our weakness" (Rom. 8:26). Trusting in Him, we can continue our dialogue, we can tackle the acts required of us.

Let us begin with the most important dialogue, with the most important act, let us pray! Before the incomprehensible grace of God, let us pray with the Apostle of the Gentiles: ''O the depth of the riches and wisdom and knowledge of God! How unsearchable are his judgments and how inscrutable his ways! For who has known the mind of the Lord, or who has been his counsellor? Or who has given a gift to him that he might be repaid? For from him and through him and to him are all things. To him be glory for ever. Amen'' (Rom. 11:33-36).

A RENEWAL OF CHRISTIAN LIFE IS NEEDED FOR UNITY

After the meeting with the representatives of the Evangelical Church on Monday morning, November 17, the Holy Father received the representatives of the other Christian denominations present in Germany. The Pope delivered the following address.

Venerated brothers and sisters in Christ,

"How good and pleasant it is when brothers dwell in unity!" (Ps. 133:1) Can we not all experience anew the truth of these words of the psalm at this hour? We have found ourselves together as *brothers in the Lord.* Brotherhood is not an empty word or a fleeting dream for us; it is a happy reality, today and here and wherever Christians obey their Lord and follow Him. The grace of God unites us with Him and with one another. We can be confident with Vatican II that "the bond of brotherhood existing among all Christians...leads toward full and perfect unity, in accordance with what God in His kindness wills" (*Unitatis redintegratio,* no. 5). We are all destined to live together in the one "family of God"; we are called "to save and renew every creature, so that all things might be restored in Christ, and so that in Him men might form one family and one People of God" (*Ad gentes,* no. 1).

All the joy for our meeting, for our vocation and mission, must not make us forget how little we have responded and respond to the grace of God. In spite of our deep union, we are, in fact, divided in many things.

Our being together in your German homeland confronts us with the event of the Reformation. We must think of what preceded it and of what has happened since. If we do not evade the facts, we realize that the faults of men led to the unhappy division of Christians, and that our faults again hinder the possible and necessary steps towards unity. I emphatically make my own what my Predecessor Hadrian VI said in 1523 at the Diet of Nuremberg: "Certainly the Lord's hand has not been shortened so much that He cannot save us, but sin separates us from Him.... All of us, prelates and priests, have strayed from the right path and there is not anyone who does good (cf. Ps. 14:3). Therefore, we must all render honor to God and humble ourselves before Him. Each of us must consider why he has fallen and judge himself rather than be judged by God on the day of wrath." With the last German or Dutch Pope, I say: "The disease is deep-rooted and developed; we must therefore proceed step by step, and first of all treat the most serious and dangerous ills with suitable medicines, so as not to make things even more confused with a hasty reform." Today, as then, the first and most important step towards unity is the renewal of Christian life. "There can be no ecumenism worthy of the name without interior conversion" (*Unitatis redintegratio*, no. 7).

In the effort for renewal and union, much of what has already been done in your country from the ecumenical point of view can help us. Among these things are the coming together of separated brothers in the years of calamities and tribulations suffered in common, the martyrdom of those who sacrificed their lives for unity in Christ, the common scientific efforts made together for decades for the unity of Christians, the ecumenical translation of Holy Scripture made together, reciprocal and regular official contacts, the efforts made again and again to meet together the challenges of our time, reflection, animated by an ecumenical spirit, on the intention and testimony of the *Confessio Augustana* and the celebration of its 450th anniversary, union in the Workers' Association of Christian Churches (ACK) "for common witness and service" (par. 1 of the ACK statute).

God be thanked for all this! May He grant everyone strength and courage not to relax the numerous efforts for full union. May He grant that the good seed will grow and yield abundant fruit!

Certainly everything depends decisively on our uniting more and more "for common witness and service." The unity of the Church undeniably belongs to her essence. She is not an end in herself. The Lord gives her "that the world may believe" (Jn. 17:21). Let us do everything in our power to bear witness together to what is given to us in Jesus Christ.

He is the "one mediator between God and men" (1 Tim. 2:5). "There is salvation in no one else" (Acts 4:12). All steps towards the center oblige us and encourage us at the same time to venture to take the necessary steps towards all our sisters and brothers. Like the love of the Lord, so, too, real service following Him knows no limits. It concerns all the dimensions of human existence and all the spheres of our

time. Let us contribute together "to a just appreciation of the dignity of the human person, to the promotion of the blessings of peace, the application of
Gospel principles to social life, and the advancement
of the arts and sciences in a truly Christian spirit...to
use every possible means to relieve the afflictions of
our times, such as famine and natural disasters, il-
literacy and poverty, lack of housing, and the unequal
distribution of wealth" (*Unitatis redintegratio,* no. 12).

Recalling this requirement of the Decree on
Ecumenism, I would like to refer also to its last
words. Aware that "the reconciliation of all Christians in the unity of the one and only Church of
Christ transcends human powers and gifts," the
Council places "its hope entirely in the prayer of
Christ for the Church, in the love of the Father for us,
and in the power of the Holy Spirit. 'And hope does
not disappoint, because God's love has been poured
forth in our hearts through the Holy Spirit who has
been given to us' (Rom. 5:5)" (*Unitatis redintegratio,*
no. 24).

Let us pray: Lord, give us the power of hope, the
fire of love, the light of faith. Let us pray together as
the Lord taught us:

"Our Father...."

BUILD BRIDGES
BETWEEN
THE ETHNIC GROUPS

In the late morning of Monday, November 17, the Holy Father met representatives of immigrant workers in the Federal Republic of Germany in front of Mainz Cathedral. The Pope delivered the following address in German.

Beloved brothers and sisters,

This morning I am very happy to be with you who have come to Germany from so many countries and so many continents to work here, to study, or to make a new life for yourselves and your families.

1. The place of our meeting, the city of Mainz, already reminds us through its own history of the fundamental theme of this meeting: *"Men on the way."* Mainz is one of the very ancient cities that was founded on the banks of the Rhine with the spread of the ancient Roman Empire. Together with the soldiers and merchants, Christianity, too, came for the first time to this country from Italy. Already in the year 200 there is evidence of a Christian community in Mainz with a bishop. When later, in the eighth century, Anglo-Saxon missionaries—this time, therefore, from the north—began to spread the Faith energetically among the Germanic tribes, one of them, the great Boniface, became bishop of Mainz. Starting from here, together with his disciples, he founded many other bishoprics as far as Chur in the south and

Prague and Olmütz in the east. In his turn, the holy Bishop Adalbert brought the light of the Good News from Prague to Poland and to the Baltic countries. Yes, it is true: this city with its Romanesque cathedral with its six towers speaks to us of the foundation and of the spiritual roots of many of our countries; it speaks to us of the power of our Catholic Faith, which unites and points out the way. And this faith always found its way to the hearts of our forefathers through "men on the way," missionaries, men and women, who set out from their native lands to seek new possibilities of life in other countries, which were often completely unknown to them, and at the same time to bear witness with their life and their words to the liberating message of our redemption in Jesus Christ.

Divine Providence has called me too from my country. With election by the Cardinals to the highest pastoral office, there has been conferred on me in particular responsibility for the unity of the Church. I, too, have often been, like you, a traveler in distant lands. For this reason I greet with great understanding and particular cordiality all of you gathered here in this square, and also those of you who are united with us through radio and television, or who will be informed of our meeting later. May the peace of the Lord be with you all!

FOREIGN WORKERS' LIVES FULL OF DIFFICULTIES

2. It was not an easy decision for you, dear brothers and sisters, to set out from your native lands to seek work and better possibilities of life, for you

and the members of your family, here in the Federal Republic of Germany. You ventured to take this step because you had the well-founded hope that the people of the country that was to give you hospitality would treat you with understanding and accept you with social justice and Christian charity. May this expectation have been met to some extent for as many of you as possible! In the meantime, you have carried out great and important works in this country with your hands, for the benefit of all men, and for this you have won recognition and respect. Many of you have already been in Germany for five, ten years, or longer, and feel almost at home, especially your children and young people who were born here.

The life of a foreign worker is also, however, bound up with great problems and difficulties. Your spokesman has already recalled them in his greeting. Many do not know how much longer they will be able to live and work here, and they suffer from this insecurity. Many had to leave their families in the homeland, at least for the first period. When finally after great effort they succeed in bringing their wives, children and parents here, it is often difficult for them to find a decent house. Difficulties arise with regard to the adequate completion of their children's studies and to finding them a job. Above all, however, you suffer from the fact that you really do not know how to remain faithful with heart and soul to the culture of your native land with its customs and uses, with its language and its songs, and at the same time adapt yourselves to the lifestyle of your new environment. You certainly do not want to become uprooted persons, detached from your spiritual roots in the old country and not yet having grown roots in the new one. Your Catholic Faith and your religious life in particular would be jeopardized; it would be difficult or even impossible for you to introduce your children, already within the family, to the fundamental truths of faith and to the life of the Church.

Dear brothers and sisters, I am clearly aware of these important problems of your everyday life, and I know that many leaders of the Church and of the state are constantly endeavoring, together with your representatives, to alleviate individual difficulties, plan lasting solutions for everyone, and put them into practice.

FAMILY HAS PRIORITY

3. But what can you already do yourselves? Begin with your family! Respect and love your wives, your husbands, as the most important and precious persons you know! Be faithful to them unreservedly and in all matters! Let your parents and your children participate in the same way in this firm unity of sure love and natural solidarity. In this way you will have in your family a little—but living and strong—core of community, a part of your homeland for body and for soul, a place of shelter and recognition, which cannot be entirely replaced by anything else. You yourselves have already experienced this in many ways in your own countries: where the administration of the state is inadequate or lacking, where social assistance is insufficiently developed, there is still the family, which helps to find a way out of the difficulty, or at least bears the weight of the difficulty together. The same holds true here, in your new environment of life, with its mysteries and uncertainties.

I address particularly the young people among you: make good use of the possibilities of formation that are offered to you; help the older members of your families with the new knowledge you have acquired, above all as regards the language. Let your parents feel that you understand them and esteem them, even if perhaps you get along better than they do in the new country! Think highly of their origin, their culture, their mother tongue and their native dialect! They have coped with many difficulties and very courageously taken a step through which your life should become fuller and richer. But in the joy of economic advantages, do not forget the spiritual values of culture and faith; only through them will you make real progress with regard to your personality and your humanity.

I would like to encourage you all, however, to draw closer to one another: among the different ethnic groups and also individual German fellow-citizens; try to understand one another, to open up your lives to one another with all their joys and concerns. Make an effort to build bridges between the ethnic groups, stone by stone and patiently! Many little steps, taken in the same direction, may bring you closer to one another in the end, and even make you friends and bring your respective families into cordial contact.

GERMANY'S CONTRIBUTION

4. I would now like to address also the native population of this country. In the last twenty years you have not only enjoyed the economic advantages of millions of foreign workers, but you have helped

I address particularly the young people among you: make good use of the possibilities of formation that are offered to you; help the older members of your families with the new knowledge you have acquired, above all as regards the language. Let your parents feel that you understand them and esteem them, even if perhaps you get along better than they do in the new country! Think highly of their origin, their culture, their mother tongue and their native dialect! They have coped with many difficulties and very courageously taken a step through which your life should become fuller and richer.

them to benefit from the many social and juridical provisions in this country, to bring their families here and send their children to your schools. You have also tried to appreciate the particular difficulties of your guests; many of you have endeavored to drive home these requirements to your fellow-citizens at many levels. The charitable institutes of the Christian churches of Germany have also made a great contribution to these efforts. All that has been done up to now in this field deserves our gratitude and our recognition.

The development up to now, however, shows that an even greater change of mentality would be desirable in a large part of the native population. Many persons have believed for too long that the foreign workers would stay only temporarily in the industrial areas; their presence was evaluated almost exclusively on the economic level, as a question of the labor market. Now, however, it is clear to every discerning observer that a large percentage of these workers and their families feel at home here and would like to live in your country always. This means a deep change for the structure of life and of population in the Federal Republic of Germany, like several other countries of Western Europe. Politics, economics and society must take that into account; everyone must adapt himself to it in outlook and in action—a process that cannot be carried out easily or rapidly. I know that the Catholic Church in Germany is ready to make its energetic contribution. In this connection, the decision of the common Synod of Bishops in the Federal Republic of Germany in 1973 is certainly a good foundation for this. In all these efforts it must always be a question of judging the people from other countries who work in your land not just as workers according to the economic yardstick, but to see behind them the fellow man with his dignity and his rights, with his concern for his family, with his claim to be taken seriously in all areas of his life and to obtain a just share of the common good.

INCREASING EFFORTS NEEDED

5. Certainly, the starting point of all the helpful attempts to find a solution has recently worsened in a threatening way: economic development in the industrialized countries is stagnant, new streams of refugees are pouring into many nations and across many seas in search of countries that will give them shelter, and countless other men feel persecuted or discriminated against on the political level and seek an asylum where they will be able to breathe freely. Millions of people see starvation staring them in the face at this very moment. This situation will require such increasing efforts on the part of those in charge that the limit of what is reasonable and of what is attainable will very soon appear. This point has not yet come, but we must prepare for it in our minds. Is this not a challenge to politicians, a challenge that should be met in a common effort, beyond the interests of parties and countries? Above all it is necessary to look out carefully for any signs of xenophobia, in order to be able—also through the mass media and all those who form public opinion—to combat blind feelings of anxiety and instinctive reactions of defense with a concrete realism which is courageous enough to declare that the age of unlimited development is over, and to prepare the population for a necessary limitation of the possibilities of life for individuals. In the

long run, no well-off country will be able to defend itself from the attack of so many men who have little or nothing to live on.

Probably it will be less and less possible in the future for the individual citizen to live in his own country without bothering about his neighbor who comes from abroad, and to leave to social welfare offices and charitable institutions the task of meeting his needs. Everyone must examine his own attitude toward the foreigners who are near him and verify in all conscience whether he has already discovered in them men with the same longing for peace and freedom, tranquility and security, the satisfaction of which we claim for ourselves as a matter of course.

CHURCH'S CONSTANT
AND COMPLETE COMMITMENT

6. The Catholic Church as a whole, and also the individual local churches in the various countries, are well aware of this task, which calls for a constant and complete commitment. You know, dear brothers and sisters, that the Church has long put at the disposal of those of you who are Christians a house for your faith and protection for your human rights, appointing pastors of souls from your respective homelands who help you to live and bear witness to your faith even in a new environment. The Church has set up welfare centers which advise you in juridical questions and supply you with ready assistance in cases of necessity. Today I would like to address a sincere word of thanks and gratitude to this host of priests, sisters and lay assistants who stand by your side, charged by Christ and His Church. You

have taken upon yourselves the destiny of living abroad, in order to be a support in faith for your compatriots; like good shepherds you have followed the flock to protect it. In this way you live following Christ, the Good Shepherd. He will bless and reward your efforts! At the same time I would like to encourage you to continue to collaborate trustfully with the German dioceses and to dedicate your loving concern together with the native priests and religious. This is, after all, where you must lead your flock: to the communion of Catholic Christians, as it appears locally in the parish community, which offers space for a multiplicity of men, gathered in the same faith in our Lord Jesus Christ.

But not all the guests of this country are Christians; a particularly large group profess the faith of Islam. My blessing goes to you, too, from the bottom of my heart! If you have sincerely brought your faith in God from your country to a foreign land and pray to God here as your Creator and Lord, you too belong to the great host of pilgrims who, since Abraham, have set out again and again to seek and find the true God. When you are not ashamed to pray even in public, in this way you set us Christians an example worthy of the utmost respect. Live your faith also in a foreign land and do not let it be exploited by any human or political interest!

EXPERIENCE
OF REAL CATHOLICITY

7. Dear brothers and sisters!

I hope that most of you have already mastered the German language enough to be able to understand my words. They came from the heart and understanding of the Supreme Pastor of the Church, who knows how difficult a life far from one's country can be, but who is also convinced how much unifying and saving power our Catholic Faith contains, in order that you may be able to acquire a new homeland among your brothers and sisters in faith who belong to this country. Certainly, the meeting of Christians with such a fullness of different forms of expression of the same faith can lead even to an enrichment of all the participants, to new amazement at the fullness of God, who is reflected, still incompletely, yet already so richly, in the Church which lives as *one* among *many* peoples. May the witness of faith of all of us be so living and powerful that this splendid experience of real catholicity will be given to us again and again!

In Italian

I am happy to address now a special greeting to you, dear Italian workers in Germany, who certainly keep alive in your hearts the thought of your country of origin, bringing with you its familiar noble traditions, woven with human and religious values, which cannot fail to contribute also to the welfare of your host country.

You, in fact, while you contribute to the economic development of this nation, aspire at the same time to be welcomed as persons and to be fully integrated in the social life of this people (cf. *Gaudium et spes*, no. 66). It is clear, however, that these legitimate intentions are accompanied by as many duties: of honesty, industry, collaboration, and friendly coexistence. Now the serene and persevering exercise of these responsibilities finds prevalent support and nourishment in faith.

In this connection, I wish to address to you a threefold fatherly exhortation. In the first place, make the family structure stronger, defending it from the many recurrent dangers, aware that life buds and grows within the domestic walls, and that the real happiness of the couple likewise matures. Support, furthermore, the work of your priests with constant participation in Sunday Mass and at the various meetings for religious instruction. Feel more and more that you are an Upper Room of believers who, in prayer and brotherhood, travel together along the earthly way towards endless life. Lastly, revive every day your devotion to the Blessed Virgin, so venerated in every region and village in your Italy, and whom you have learned to love from your childhood, often a troubled one. While I greet you cordially, I entrust to Mary your thoughts, your plans, and your families.

In Spanish

At this meeting in the square of Mainz Cathedral, I cannot fail to greet you with great affection, dear Spanish workers of this city and of the whole Federal Republic of Germany. It is a greeting that I willingly extend to your wives and children, whether they live with you or are far away.

I am well aware that your condition as immigrants puts you in particular circumstances which sometimes entail great efforts and sacrifices for yourselves and for your families. For this reason I wish to tell you that I understand and share your anxieties and hopes as persons trying honestly to construct a better future for yourselves and for your families.

Allow me to encourage you not to reduce this noble task only to the material or economic sphere, but to extend it also to the spiritual and religious sphere. In fact, it is your whole person, as men and Christians, that bears within it a peculiar dignity, which derives from the sublime vocation to which God calls you. Be faithful, therefore, to these values that you received in your places of origin and that you must develop now, in a spirit of mutual solidarity. This will make you the first promoters of yourselves, opening you to all others. Addressing you, priests and men and women religious who assist the immigrants, I call upon you to consider the great importance and ecclesial and human value of your mission, a difficult but valuable one. So do not let yourselves be discouraged by difficulties. And rest assured, all of you, that the Pope always accompanies you with prayer and blesses you.

In Slovene

A cordial greeting to you, too, dear Slovenes, who live and work heré.

I urge you: remain faithful to your country and to its rich spiritual and cultural traditions. Bear witness with your whole life to your faith and honesty. Be open at the same time to the values offered to you —though sometimes through trials—by the land that gives you hospitality. Enrich your spirit with them, too.

May my blessing reach you, beloved in Christ, your families at home and abroad, and your pastors of souls.

God be with you all!

In Croatian

My dear Croats!

I am happy to greet you, too, who live here in Germany in such great numbers. While you work here, let your thoughts be close to your parents, your families, your children, who have remained in Croatia and think of you so much and pray for you. Always be faithful to them! With your attendance at Church and with observance of the Sunday precept, continue to be an example to other Catholics of this country. Repeating the words of the Psalmist, who prayed: "If I forget you, O Jerusalem, let my right hand wither!" (Ps. 137:5), you, too, say: "Let my right hand wither should I forget my holy Church, my family, and my Croat people!"

May my blessing accompany each of you and all your families.

THE RICHNESS OF OUR COMMON HERITAGE

The Pope's last meeting in Mainz, on the morning of Monday, November 17, was with representatives of the Jewish community. He delivered the following address.

Shalom!

Ladies and gentlemen, dear brothers and sisters!

I thank you for your friendly and sincere words of greeting. This meeting was a deep need for me in the framework of this apostolic journey, and I thank you for fulfilling it. May God's blessing accompany this hour!

1. If Christians must consider themselves brothers of all men and behave accordingly, this holy obligation is all the more binding when they find themselves before members of the Jewish people! In the "Declaration on the Relationship of the Church with Judaism" in April of this year, the Bishops of the Federal Republic of Germany put this sentence at the beginning: "Whoever meets Jesus Christ, meets Judaism." I would like to make these words mine, too. The faith of the Church in Jesus Christ, the son of David and the son of Abraham (cf. Mt. 1:1), actually contains what the Bishops call in that declaration "the

spiritual heritage of Israel for the Church" (par. 11), a living heritage, which must be understood and preserved in its depth and richness by us Catholic Christians.

GRATEFUL ADMIRATION

2. The concrete brotherly relations between Jews and Catholics in Germany assume a quite particular value against the grim background of the persecution and the attempted extermination of Judaism in this country. The innocent victims in Germany and elsewhere, the families destroyed or dispersed, the cultural values or art treasures destroyed forever, are a tragic proof where discrimination and contempt of human dignity can lead, especially if they are animated by perverse theories on a presumed difference in the value of races or on the division of men into men of "high worth," "worthy of living," and men who are "worthless," "unworthy of living." Before God all men are of the same value and importance.

In this spirit, during the persecution, Christians likewise committed themselves, often at the risk of their lives, to prevent or relieve the sufferings of their Jewish brothers and sisters. I would like to express recognition and gratitude to them at this moment. And also to those people who, as Christians, affirming they belonged to the Jewish people, travelled along the *via crucis* of their brothers and sisters to the end—like the great Edith Stein, called in her religious institute Teresa Benedikta of the Cross, whose memory is rightly held in great honor.

I would further like to mention also Franz Rosenzweig and Martin Buber, who, through their creative familiarity with the Jewish and German languages, constructed a wonderful bridge for a deeper meeting of both cultural areas.

You yourselves stressed, in your words of greeting, that in the many efforts to build up a new common life with Jewish citizens in this country, Catholics and the Church have made a decisive contribution. This recognition and the necessary collaboration on your part fills me with joy. For my part, I wish to express grateful admiration also for your initiatives in this connection, including the recent foundation of your Heidelberg University.

TRUSTING COLLABORATION

3. The depth and richness of our common heritage are revealed to us particularly in friendly dialogue and trusting collaboration. I rejoice that, in this country, conscious and zealous care is dedicated to all this. Many public and private initiatives in the pastoral, academic, and social fields serve this purpose, as on very solemn occasions such as the recent one at the Katholikentag in Berlin. Also an encouraging sign was the meeting of the international liaison committee between the Roman Catholic Church and Judaism in Regensburg last year.

It is not just a question of correcting a false religious view of the Jewish people, which in the course of history was one of the causes that contributed to misunderstanding and persecution, but above all of the dialogue between the two religions which—with

May He, the ineffable of whom His creation speaks to us: He, who does not force mankind to goodness, but guides it; He, who manifests Himself in our fate and is silent; He, who chooses all of us as His people; may He guide us along His ways to His future!

Praised be His Name! Amen.

Islam—gave the world faith in the one, ineffable God who speaks to us, and which desire to serve Him on behalf of the whole world.

The first dimension of this dialogue, that is, the meeting between the People of God of the Old Covenant, never revoked by God (cf. Rom. 11:29), and that of the New Covenant, is at the same time a dialogue within our Church, that is to say, between the first and the second part of her Bible. In this connection the directives for the application of the conciliar Declaration *Nostra aetate* say: "The effort must be made to understand better everything in the Old Testament that has its own, permanent value..., since this value is not wiped out by the later interpretation of the New Testament, which, on the contrary, gave the Old Testament its full meaning, so that it is a question rather of reciprocal enlightenment and explanation" (no. 11).

A second dimension of our dialogue—the true and central one—is the meeting between the present-day Christian Churches and the present-day people of the covenant concluded with Moses. It is important here "that Christians"—so continue the post-conciliar directives—"should aim at understanding better the fundamental elements of the religious tradition of Judaism, and learn what fundamental lines are essential for the religious reality lived by the Jews, according to their own understanding" (Introduction). The way for this mutual knowledge is dialogue. I thank you, venerated brothers and sisters, for carrying it out, you too, with that "openness and breadth of spirit," with that "tact" and with that "prudence" which are recommended to us Catholics by the above-mentioned directives. A fruit of this dialogue and an indication for its fruitful continuation is the declaration of German bishops quoted at the beginning "on the relationship between the Church and Judaism" in April of this year. It is my eager desire that this declaration should become the spiritual property of all Catholics in Germany!

I would also like to refer briefly to a third dimension of our dialogue. The German bishops dedicated the concluding chapter of their declaration to the tasks which we have in common. Jews and Christians, as children of Abraham, are called to be a blessing for the world (cf. Gen. 12:2ff.), by committing themselves together for peace and justice among all men and peoples, with the fullness and depth that God Himself intended us to have, and with the readiness for sacrifices that this high goal may demand. The more our meeting is imprinted with this sacred duty, the more it becomes a blessing also for ourselves.

FOR THE FULLNESS OF "SHALOM"

4. In the light of this promise and call of Abraham's, I look with you to the destiny and role of your people among the peoples. I willingly pray with you for the fullness of Shalom for all your brothers in nationality and in faith, and also for the land to which Jews look with particular veneration. Our century saw the first pilgrimage of a Pope to the Holy Land. In conclusion, I wish to repeat Paul VI's words on entering Jerusalem: "Implore with us, in your desire and in your prayer, respect and peace upon this unique land, visited by God! Let us pray here together for the grace

of a real and deep brotherhood between all men, between all peoples!... May they who love you be blessed. Yes, may peace dwell in your walls, prosperity in your palaces. I pray for peace for you, I desire happiness for you" (cf. Ps. 122:6-9).

May all peoples in Jerusalem soon be reconciled and blessed in Abraham! May He, the ineffable of whom His creation speaks to us; He, who does not force mankind to goodness, but guides it; He, who manifests Himself in our fate and is silent; He, who chooses all of us as His people; may He guide us along His ways to His future!

Praised be His Name! Amen.

LET US CARRY
CHRIST'S LOVE
TO A WORLD
THIRSTING FOR IT

On Monday, November 17, in Fulda's Cathedral, where St. Boniface, the Apostle of Germany, is buried, the Holy Father celebrated Mass and delivered the following homily to priests, deacons, and seminarians.

1. Dear brothers in Christ, Cardinals, archbishops and bishops, who form the Episcopate of your homeland; my priests, beloved in Christ from the College of priests of every diocesan Church in Germany; dear deacons; dear seminarians, dear students of theology:

The words of the apostle Peter which we have heard today in the second Lesson of this liturgical celebration appear to me to have a very special sound here at the tomb of St. Boniface in Fulda: "So I exhort the elders among you, as a fellow elder and a witness of the sufferings of Christ, as well as a partaker in the glory that is to be revealed: Tend the flock of God that is your charge, taking care of it" (1 Pt. 5:1-2).

Nineteen hundred years have already passed since these words were written, and yet they still have the same freshness and force. They seem to me even to proclaim a very special message at this moment during your presence at the tomb of the bishop and martyr who is Germany's principal patron saint, precisely you to whom Peter's appeal is directed, certainly in different degrees: "Take care of the flock of God." Peter, who was the first to be called upon by the Good Shepherd to perform this task: "Feed my sheep" (Jn. 21:16), addresses himself as one of the "elders" to all those who, together with him, were shepherds of his time. With what deep emotion do we who are today shepherds of the Church hear these words, in the second millennium of Christianity which is drawing to its close! You who, according to the different ranks of your ministry, bishops, priests, or deacons, are shepherds of the Church in your homeland! And also you who have answered Christ's vocation and are preparing yourselves for your ministry as shepherds in time to come!

"Take care of the flock of God." Be shepherds of your brothers and sisters in your faith, your Baptismal grace, and your hope of sacred participation in the eternal grace and love!

ROOTED IN THE MYSTERY OF CHRIST

2. Peter reminds us in his Epistle of the suffering of Christ and likewise of the mystery of Easter to which he became a witness. With that testimony of

the cross and the resurrection he then also links the hope of being "a partaker of that glory which is to be revealed" (1 Pt. 5:1).

The vocation to become shepherds of the Church and their various pastoral services always and everywhere have their roots in the comprehensive mystery of Christ: they lead from Him and to Him; in Him they find the strength for growth and full support; they serve Him with the fruit of their labor.

This mystery is then believed in true faith if those who serve Him are like men "who wait for their Lord when he shall return from the wedding, that when he comes and knocks they may open immediately" (Lk. 12:36).

It is therefore the service of being alert for the Lord.

When Jesus began His time of suffering He took the Apostles with Him into the Garden of Gethsemane. Three of them He led even deeper into the garden and asked them to watch with Him. But when, overcome with tiredness, they had fallen asleep, He returned to them and said: "Watch, and pray that you enter not into temptation" (Mt. 27:41).

Thus the service we are performing, dear brothers, is that of watching for the Lord. Watching means waiting beside that with which we have been entrusted. And that possession with which we have been entrusted is infinitely precious. We must constantly keep watch over it. We must submerge the roots of our faith, of our hope and love ever more in the "wonderful works of God" (Acts 2:11); we must identify ourselves ever more with the Revelation of the Father in Christ; and finally, we must be ever more sensitive to the influence of the Holy Spirit whom the Lord has bestowed upon us and whom we want to keep on bestowing upon us through our ministry, through our holiness, through our priestly identity.

In the same way we must develop an ever deeper feeling for the greatness of man as revealed to us in the mystery of the Incarnation and the Redemption: how precious is every human soul and how rich the treasures of grace and love.

Then we shall be able to act in accordance with Peter's exhortation, who has urged us to perform our duties "not by constraint but willingly, according to God...eagerly...being examples to the flock" (1 Pt. 5:2-3).

GREAT MEN OF GOD

3. Let us consider the many outstanding bishops and priests whom this country has produced. I will name only a few of more recent times: Bishop von Ketteler and Adolf Kolping; Cardinals von Galen, Frings, Döpfner and Bengsch; Father Alfred Delp and the young priest, Karl Leisner; Karl Sonnenschein and Father Rupert Mayer; Romani Guardini and Father Kentenich.

Let us study them more closely! They all show us the meaning of this "watching"; what it means to have "one's loins girt" and to carry "lamps burning in your hands" (Lk. 12:35); how one can be a "faithful and wise servant, whom his master has set over his household to give them their food at the proper time" (Mt. 24:45).

These and many other model priests of the Church in your country can show us how our calling and all our ministry as bishops, priests or deacons are based on that glorious mystery of the human heart: the mystery of friendship with Christ, and how through the strength of that friendship the shepherd's true love of man grows, a mature, selfless love, which the world today thirsts for so greatly, and especially the young generation.

I know that countless priests of the Church in your country experience the joy and the happiness of this deep spiritual affinity with Jesus Christ. But I also know that there are also hours of anguish, of exhaustion, helplessness, and disappointment in the life of the priest today. I am convinced that this is also part of the life of those priests who devote their entire energy to the faithful accomplishment of their mission and perform their duties with great conscientiousness. Should it come as a surprise to us that the one who in his mission is so closely linked with Jesus Christ also shares the hours Jesus spent on the Mount of Olives?

FRIENDSHIP WITH CHRIST

4. What medicine can I offer you in this situation? Not that you should increase your activities, not that you should make desperate efforts, but that you should hold deeper communion with yourselves with regard to your calling, that very friendship with Christ, friendship with one another. Through you Christ Himself wants to be visible as the friend of all in your midst and in the midst of your parishes. "No longer do I call you servants,...but I have called you friends" (Jn. 15:15).

These words, which still resound in your hearts from the time of your ordination, should be the keynote of your life. To my friend I can say anything, I can confide my private thoughts with him: all my troubles and sorrows, all the unresolved problems and painful experiences.

I can base my life on His words, on the sacraments of the Eucharist and, not least, of Penance. That is the ground on which we stand. Have trust in Jesus Christ that He may not leave you, that He will assist you in the performance of your duties, even at times when success does not immediately appear to be at hand. Believe that although He expects everything of you, He does so as a friend expects it of his friends.

Friendship with Jesus Christ: that is also the deepest reason why a life of celibacy, indeed taken as a whole in the spirit of the evangelical counsels, is so important for the priest. To have one's heart and one's hands free for our friend Jesus Christ, to be totally at His disposal and to carry His love to all men—that is a testimony which is not immediately understood by all. But if we inwardly fulfill that testimony, if we live it as our friendship with Jesus, then the understanding for this lifestyle which has its foundations in the Gospel will grow again in the community.

Friendship with Jesus has as both its fruit and consequence friendship with one another. The priests form a college around their bishop. The bishop is the one who represents Christ in a special way for you and with you. He who is a friend of Christ cannot bypass the mission of the bishop. Indeed, he will sense it; he will not pit his own views and standards against the mission which Christ has given the bishop. Unity with the bishop and the unity with the successor of Peter are the firm foundation of a fidelity which cannot be lived without the friendship of Christ. That union is also essential if our ministry, the ministry of the bishops and the Pope, is to be performed in open, fraternal and understanding affection for you.

But that friendship demands still more. It demands that fraternal openness for one another, that we help to carry one another's burdens. It demands a common testimony so that we do not judge one another, mistrust one another, or think of our own prestige. I am convinced that if you conduct your ministry in the spirit of friendship and fraternity, you will achieve more than if everyone goes his own way. In the strength of such a friendship with the Lord you will be able to "watch" as was the Lord's hope of the "good servants" in the Gospel.

WATCHFUL MINISTRY

5. This "being watchful" on the part of the servant—the friend—waiting for the Lord relates also to the ultimate future in God and to the course of that history, to every moment. The Lord can come "in the second watch or in the third watch" (Lk. 12:38).

Through the instructions handed down by the Second Vatican Council the whole Church has made it clear that it directs its mission in each case to the present, that is, to a world which is constantly developing, and above all to the hopes of the people in that world, to its joy and hope, but also its waywardness and errors (cf. *Gaudium et spes*, no. 1).

The ministry of the watchful and attentive shepherd also means, therefore, opening one's eyes wide to everything good and genuine, to everything true and beautiful, but also to everything grave and sorrowful in the life of man, and to do so full of love, full of readiness to be close at hand in a spirit of solidarity, even to sacrifice one's life (Jn. 10:11).

The shepherd's watchful ministry also means being ready to defend others against the ravaging wolf—as in the parable of the Good Shepherd—or against the thief that he may not break into the house (Lk. 12:39). With that I do not mean a priest who keeps a strict, distrustful and merciless eye on the flock entrusted to him, but a shepherd who aims to free his flock from sin and guilt by the offer of reconciliation, who above all grants the people the sacrament of Penance.

"For Christ," the priest may and should call out to an irreconciled and irreconcilable world: "be reconciled with God" (2 Cor. 5:20). In this way we reveal to the people the heart of God the Father and are thus an image of Christ the Good Shepherd. Our whole life can then become a sign and tool of reconciliation, the "sacrament" of the union between God and man.

But together with me you will note that the personal reception of the sacrament of Penance in your parishes has fallen off very considerably in recent years. I earnestly beseech you, indeed I admonish you, to do everything possible to make the sacrament of Penance in personal confession something which all who have been baptized will again regard as the natural thing to do. That is the aim of penitential Church services which play a very important part in the practice of the Church, but under normal circumstances cannot be a substitute for the personal reception of the sacrament of Penance. But also endeavor yourselves to receive the sacrament of Penance regularly.

LIKE THE GOOD SHEPHERD

6. The watchfulness of the Good Shepherd is expected of you in the essence of any priestly activity, the celebration of the holy liturgy. Precisely after the comprehensive reform of divine services there are important pastoral tasks for you to perform. You will yourselves first have to study and attentively practice the approved rites. You should be in a position, as liturgists, to minister to the deeper faith, the stronger hope and the greater love among the People of God. I wish to thank you for all the work you have put into the achievement of those important aims, whose good fruit I have already been privileged to see among you. It is all the more regrettable that the celebration of the Mystery of Christ, here and there, instead of spreading unity with Christ and among one another, causes dissension and division. Nothing could be more inimical to the will and the spirit of Christ.

I therefore beseech you, my priestly brothers and friends, to proceed with responsibility along the path of the Church which, true to its old tradition, it has today resolved to follow, and to keep it from any spurious subjectivism. But I should like to emphasize that the special liturgical arrangements which the German bishops have requested on pastoral grounds have been granted by the Apostolic See and are therefore legitimate.

God, You are wondrous in Your saints!

Appointed by You to the highest pastoral office of the Church of Jesus Christ, I kneel today as a pilgrim at the tomb of St. Albert, to glorify You with all the faithful on this day commemorating the 700th anniversary of his death, and to thank You for his life and his works, through which You gave him to Your Church as a teacher of the faith and an example of Christian life.

Arturo Mari

Dear young people, you have been called, called by God. My life, my human life is only meaningful if I have been called by God, in an important, decisive, final call. Only God can call man this way, no one but He. And this call of God constantly goes out, in and through Christ, to each and every one of you: To be workers in the harvest of your own humanity, workers in the vineyards of the Lord, in the Messianic harvest of humanity.

Felici

Jesus is in need of young people from your ranks who will follow His call and live as He did, poor and celibate, in order to be a living sign of the reality of God among your brothers and sisters.

St. Boniface, bishop and martyr, means the "beginning" of the Gospel and of the Church in your country. We have come here today to follow on from that beginning, in order to open up his dimensions for ourselves. The "beginning" means the work of God Himself who used the testimony of man for His purpose: the testimony of Boniface, of his life and his martyrdom.

Felici

   This kingdom of God is in our midst (cf. Lk. 17:21),
as it was in all the generations of your fathers and
ancestors. But like them, we too still pray in the "Our
Father" every day: "Thy kingdom come." These words
bear witness that the kingdom of God is still ahead of
us, that we are moving towards it, advancing along the
confused paths, and in fact sometimes even the wrong
ones, of our earthly existence.

And now allow me to turn again to St. Albert the Great, the celebration of whose seventh centenary has brought me to your city. Here, in fact, is the tomb of this famous son of your country, who was born in Lauingen, and in his long life was at once a great scientist, a spiritual son of St. Dominic, and the teacher of Saint Thomas Aquinas. He was one of the greatest intellects of the thirteenth century. More than any other, he wove the "net" that unites faith and reason, God's wisdom and worldly knowledge.

Respect and love your wives, your husbands, as the most important and precious persons you know! Be faithful to them unreservedly and in all matters! Let your parents and your children participate in the same way in this firm unity of sure love and natural solidarity. In this way you will have in your family a little—but living and strong—core of community.

Arturo Mari

Be convinced and convincing Christians today! May the present renewal of your magnificent house of God be an appeal to you. We, too, the living stones of the spiritual temple of the Church, must always renew ourselves in Jesus Christ, until we are fully conformed to Him.

Arturo Mari

I urge you: remain faithful to your country and to its rich spiritual and cultural traditions. Bear witness with your whole life to your faith and honesty.

Felici

It is just believing in the fact that the love of Christ is stronger that can give us the unabashed strength to stand up against indifference, resignation, helplessness, fear of life, and cynicism, and for the unshortened message of the Gospel. At those places where we act like that, where we clearly and directly preach the Gospel and underline it by our way of living, people will listen very attentively. This applies to young people in particular. We have to create living cells in which believing people pass on and exemplify through their own life how relieving it is to be in the imitation of Christ.

When the Lord's bread is broken and His body offered in Holy Communion, we live and realize in a clear and perceptible way this deep unity of the body of Christ, the communion of all believers. Gain a new awareness today, in joyful gratitude, of this deep and intimate union of the whole Church beyond all human boundaries and barriers! Take away this awareness as a precious treasure to your communities, to your neighborhoods, to your families!

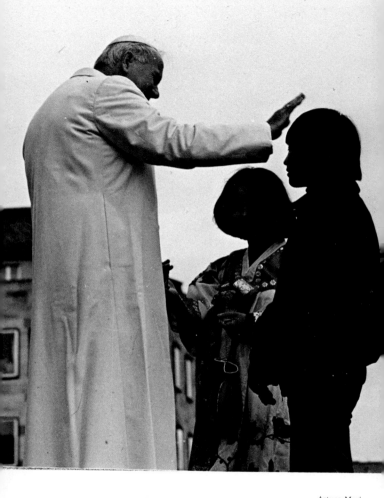

Arturo Mari

I would like to encourage you all to draw closer to one another: among the different ethnic groups and also individual German fellow-citizens; try to understand one another, to open up your lives to one another with all their joys and concerns. Make an effort to build bridges between the ethnic groups, stone by stone and patiently!

Arturo Mari

Be holy! Yes, sanctify your own life and keep in
your midst the one who alone is holy. Only if you
make the unmistakable characteristics of the Gospel
the focal point of your life will you be able to inspire
and attract people. And in your world mission promote the sanctification of the world.

Felici

Marriage is geared to duration, to the future. It looks beyond itself. Marriage alone is suitable for procreation and the upbringing of children. Therefore, matrimonial love is by its very nature geared also to fertility. In this role of handing down life, spouses are coliaborators with the love of God the Creator.

Arturo Mari

The Pope bows with devotion before old age, and he invites all people to do the same with him. Old age is the crown of the steps of life. It gathers in the harvest, the harvest from what you have learned and experienced, the harvest from what you have done and achieved, the harvest from what you have suffered and undergone.

Felici

I can still see before me the exultant crowd, thousands of faithful Christians in silent prayer, who wanted to pay a tribute of devotion to the Successor of St. Peter, thereby reaffirming their sentiments of profound communion with the Apostolic See that Christ wanted to be a firm foundation of truth and unity.

Endeavor above all to proclaim the teaching of Jesus Christ in union with the entire community of the Church in a reverent and faithful celebration of the Mass, Jesus Christ with whom you yourselves are united in friendship.

UNDERSTANDING YOUR CALL AND MISSION

7. Dear brothers, dear sons in the Lord!

How deeply must we love our ministry and our calling! This I say to you all, to the older ones among you who are perhaps already tired and exhausted under the burden of your work; to those of you who are in the prime of their energy; and to those of you who are about to enter the priesthood. And I am also addressing the younger ones who hear God's secret calling. I want to encourage you to bring that vocation more firmly and more deeply into your lives and to follow it irrevocably and forever.

Today's first Lesson from the prophet Jeremiah speaks very clearly of the miracle of that calling. An unprecedented but real dialogue between God and man. God-Jahweh says: "Before I formed you in the womb, I knew you: and before you were born, I consecrated you; I appointed you a prophet to the nations."

Man-Jeremiah replies: "Ah, Lord God, behold, I do not know how to speak, for I am only a youth."

God-Jahweh replies: "Do not say: 'I am only a youth'; for to all to whom I send you, you shall go, and whatever I command you, you shall speak. Be not afraid of them: for I am with you to deliver you" (Jer. 1:5-8).

How deep is the truth that lies in this dialogue! We should definitely make it the truth of our own life! We must grasp it with both hands and with our whole heart; we must live it, make it the subject of our prayers and become as one with it!

And this is at the same time the theological and psychological truth about our life! Man who perceives his calling and his mission speaks to God out of his weakness.

BE NOT AFRAID

8. The various advocates of a priesthood which differs from the image as developed by the Church and principally maintained in the Western tradition often appear today to make this weakness the fundamental principle of all else by almost declaring it to be a human right.

But Christ has taught us that man has above all a right to his greatness, a right to that which really towers above him. For it is precisely here that his special dignity emerges; here is revealed the wonderful power of grace: our true greatness is a gift deriving from the strength of the Holy Spirit.

In Christ man has a right to such greatness. And the Church, through that same Christ, has a right to the gift of man: to a gift by which man offers himself totally to God, in which he also opts for celibacy "for the kingdom of heaven" (Mt. 19:12), in order to be the servant of all.

Man and the Church have a right to this. We should not weaken this certainty and conviction within ourselves! We must not abandon this illustrious legacy of the Church, nor should we hamper its growth in the hearts of the young.

Do not abandon your trust in God and in Christ! The Lord says: "Be not afraid of them: for I am with you to deliver you" (Jer. 1:8). After these words the Lord touches man's mouth and says: "Behold, I have put my words in your mouth" (Jer. 1:9). Have we not had the same experience? Does He not, when we take Holy Orders, place His words—the words of the Eucharistic consecration—in our mouth? Does He not seal our lips and man's whole being with the power of His grace?

With us also are the saints of the Church: the patron saints of your dioceses, the great ministers of your country, the famous women of charity, and above all, Mary the Mother of the Church.

When Luke the Evangelist describes the Lord's ascension to the disciples who were "persevering with one mind" in prayer, he specifically says: "With Mary the Mother of Jesus" (Acts 1:14). She, the Mother of the Lord, the Mother of all the faithful, the Mother, too, of priests, wants to be with us so that we can ever again be sent in the Holy Spirit into this world and to the people with their troubles.

A REWARD AWAITS YOU

9. Dear brothers, dear sons in the Lord! The Lessons of this liturgy finally also tell us the reward that awaits Shepherds who stay awake. The apostle Peter speaks of the "never fading crown of glory" (1 Pt. 5:4).

But more impressive still are the words of Christ in the parable of the watchful servants: "Blessed are those servants whom the master finds awake when he comes; truly I say to you, he will gird himself and have them sit at table, and he will come and serve them. If he comes in the second watch, or in the third, and finds them so, blessed are those servants'' (Lk. 12:37-38).

I will let these words stand as they are without any addition. But may I warmly commend them to your prayers and your contemplation. Amen.

MAKE ROOM
FOR THE GIFTS
OF THE SPIRIT:
POWER, WISDOM, LOVE

In the afternoon of Monday, November 17, the Holy Father met the members of the Episcopal Conference of Germany and delivered the following address.

Dear and venerated brothers in the Episcopate!

1. Our memorable meeting today at the tomb of St. Boniface is set against the background of the great and rich history of the German people, which bears the decisive imprint of Christianity. Formed by so many forces, in the course of the centuries it has given numerous impulses of a religious, cultural and political character reaching far beyond its frontiers. I need only recall here the glorious name, pregnant with history, of the "Holy Roman Empire of the German Nation."

Your people, together with what is today the Netherlands, gave the Church seven Popes, about whom history informs us that they conscientiously carried out their service as Supreme Pastors of Christianity—even in the greatest external and internal agitations of the time. One of the main concerns common to nearly all of them during their pontificates, which were often too short, was the renewal of the Church. Special mention should be made of the zealous effort of Pope Hadrian VI for the maintenance and the re-establishment of the unity of Christians. Many of them made a personal visit as Popes to their German homeland and their former dioceses.

The interior renewal of religious and ecclesiastical life and the ecumenical effort for a rapprochement and understanding between separated Christians are the main concerns also of my apostolic journeys to the various local churches and continents. They are also the main concerns in my pastoral visit to the Church of your country and at this meeting today. The spiritual renewal of the Church and the unity of Christians are the explicit charge of the Second Vatican Council, which is equally binding on the Pope, the bishops, the priests, and the faithful. To assume joint responsibility for these tasks is the urgent imperative of the hour. They are the great challenge and the duty, above all, of our collegial responsibility as pastors of the Church. The following considerations of mine also concern them and wish to be of value to them.

From the first hour of my pontificate I understood the office of Supreme Pastor as a service for the collegiality of the bishops who are united with Peter's Successor, and conversely I understood the *"collegialitas effectiva et affectiva"* of the bishops as an important help for my own service.

On this visit to your country, I am anxious, in the first place, to express my total closeness to you, my communion with you, and to strengthen it with my witness. And here my thoughts go back to September of 1978 when I stayed here with you, in the same area of Fulda, for a brotherly exchange between the episcopate of my country, Poland, and that of your country. I am happy to see the same faces again, while at the same time my thought and my prayer go to those whom the Lord has called to Himself in the meantime. Finally I wish to greet particularly those brothers who have since then entered the college of the successors of the apostles in your country.

COMMON WITNESS

2. *Have courage for common witness.*

"If we rightly call every man, and in particular every Christian, 'brother,' " as I wrote in my letter to all brother bishops in the world on Holy Thursday, 1979, "this word assumes for us bishops and for our mutual relations a quite particular meaning: it is directly linked, in a way, with that brotherly community that united the apostles round Christ."

I am happy and grateful that, in your conference, I have already on many occasions experienced this unity with Peter's Successors and this unanimity among you. I would like to strengthen you even more in this disposition. I say to you, therefore: do not let yourselves be deceived by the often-heard opinion that a high proportion of unanimity within a conference of bishops is to the detriment of the liveliness and credibility of episcopal witness. The opposite is the case. Certainly everyone should introduce himself, in a brotherly atmosphere, without fear or reservations, and certainly everyone must contribute to build up with his contribution the unity of the body, which comprises members, services, and gifts of many kinds. But the fruitfulness of these services and gifts depends on their integration in the one life inspired by the one Spirit.

CONCERN FOR UNITY

3. *Be lovingly concerned with the unity of the presbyterate in every diocese.*

In the last few decades there have been heavy increases in what is expected and asked of priests. As a result of the decrease in the number of priests, a greater number of tasks fall upon them. The demands made on priests in their task of spiritual guidance are increased even more by the numerous professional and volunteer services of the laity in the care of souls. In a society surrounded by an ever closer network of communications, an increasingly complex spiritual dialogue becomes necessary for priests. Many priests wear themselves out in work, but become solitary and lose their bearings. It is all the more important that the unity of the presbyterate should be lived and experienced. Support everything that strengthens priests to meet one another and to help one another to live the Word and spirit of the Lord.

Three things are particularly close to my heart:

(1). The *seminaries*. They must be training-grounds of real priestly fellowship and friendship, as well as the place of a clear and solid decision for life.

(2). *Theology* must qualify for witness of faith and lead to a deepening of faith, so that priests will understand the problems of men, but also the answers of the Gospel and of the Church.

(3). Priests must receive *help* in order to meet the high requirements of celibate life and dedication to Christ and to men, and to bear witness to them through priestly simplicity, poverty, and availability. Precisely spiritual communion can render valuable services here.

THAT ALL MAY BE ONE

4. *Take seriously the prayer of the High Priest, Jesus Christ,* that all may be one, as an urgent task in order to overcome the division of Christians.

You live in the country in which the Reformation originated. Your ecclesiastical life and your social life are deeply marked by the scission of the Church, which has now lasted for over four and a half centuries. You must not resign yourselves to the fact that disciples of Christ do not give the testimony of unity before the world. Unshakable fidelity to truth, opening to others and readiness to listen to them, calm patience on the way, love and sensitivity, are necessary. Compromise does not count; what is important is only that unity which the Lord Himself founded: unity in truth and in love.

We often hear it said today that the ecumenical movement of the Churches is at a standstill, that after the spring of the changes brought by the Council, there has followed a period of coolness. In spite of many regrettable difficulties, I cannot agree with this judgment.

Unity, which comes from God, is given to us at the cross. We must not want to avoid the cross, passing to rapid attempts at harmonizing differences, excluding the question of truth. But neither must we abandon one another, and go on our separate ways, because drawing closer calls for the patient and suffering love of Christ crucified. Let us not be diverted from the laborious way in order to remain where we are, or to choose ways that are apparently shorter and lead astray.

The ecumenical way, the effort for unity, must not be limited only to the Churches born of the Reformation. Also in your country the dialogue and brotherly attitude toward other Churches and other ecclesial communities—for example, toward the Churches of Orthodoxy—are of the utmost importance. However, the memory of the *Confessio Augustana* published 450 years ago is a special appeal to the dialogue with Christianity that bears the stamp of the Reformation, and that has such a great part in the population and history of your country.

PROCLAIM THE WORD

5. *Gather the People of God, oppose false pluralism, strengthen real communion.*

I have already spoken of the high value of brotherly unity in the college of bishops and of the presbyterate. This unity, however, must be the soul by which there lives also the unity of the whole People of God in all communities. It is not a question at all of curbing or limiting the legitimate plurality of expression of spirituality, piety and theological schools. But all this must be an expression of the fullness, and not of the poverty, of faith.

The proclamation of the faith and also ecclesial life can, thank God, freely develop externally in your country. The dialogue to which you are called, however, is a demanding one. Men often find themselves spiritually in the situation of a great store in which all possible goods are praised and offered for customers to help themselves. Thus in the outlook on life of many people in your country, elements of

Christian tradition are mingled with completely different conceptions. The external freedom of saying and thinking what one likes is often confused with the inner promptings of conviction; instead of a clear orientation, indifference towards many opinions and interpretations sets in.

What are altogether your tasks and your possibilities with regard to the situation indicated?

I would like to shout two words to you. First: proclaim the Word in all clarity, indifferent to applause or rejection! It is not we, after all, who determine the success or failure of the Gospel, but the Spirit of God. Believers and non-believers have the right to hear clearly the authentic message of the Church.

Second: proclaim the Word with all the love of the Good Shepherd who dedicates Himself, searches, understands. Listen to the questions raised by those who think they can no longer find any answer in Jesus Christ and in His Church. Believe firmly that Christ Jesus is united, so to speak, with every man, and that in Him every man can rediscover himself, his real human values and questions (cf. *Gaudium et spes*, no. 22; *Redemptor hominis*, no. 13).

I would like to recommend two groups particularly to your care as pastors: in the first place those who have drawn from the impulses of the Second Vatican Council the false conclusion that the dialogue upon which the Church has entered is incompatible with the clearly obligatory character of the Magisterium and of the norms of the Church, and with the authority of the hierarchical office, founded on Christ's mission to the Church. Show that the two go together: fidelity to the indispensable mission and closeness to man with his experiences and his problems.

The other group: those who, partly as a result of inappropriate or too hasty conclusions drawn from the Second Vatican Council, no longer feel at home in the Church of today, or even threaten to break away from her. Here it is a question of transmitting to these men with the utmost decision, but at the same time with the utmost prudence, that the Church of Vatican II and that of Vatican I and of the Council of Trent and of the first Councils, is one and the same Church.

The importance of a genuine transmission of faith must not be underestimated. How grateful I am for everything that has been carried out in your country in the so-called community catechesis: believers who bear witness to faith, who transmit it to others!

The situation of faith indicated above is certainly a special challenge to priests. Will the whole heritage of faith as the Church presents it really be proclaimed everywhere in the course of a few years? Give encouragement for this; make it your responsibility. And be concerned, too, to the best of your ability, that religious instruction and catechesis will open the way to faith and life with the Church to those who often grew up in such a different background.

WITNESSING CHRISTIANITY IN DAILY LIVING

6. *Make every effort in order that the unshakable criteria and the norms of Christian action may be expressed in the lives of believers in a way as clear as it is inviting.*

Between the habits of life of a secularized society and the requirements of the Gospel, there is a deep gulf. Many people wish to take part in ecclesial life, but they no longer find any relationship between the world in which they live and Christian principles. It is believed that the Church-sticks firmly to her norms only out of obstinacy, and that this is in contradiction to that mercy of which Christ sets us the example in the Gospel. The hard demands of Jesus, His saying: "Go, and do not sin again" (Jn. 8:11), are ignored. People often fall back on personal conscience, but it is forgotten that this conscience is an eye that does not possess light by itself, but only when it looks at the real source of light.

Another thing: in the face of mechanization, functionalization and organization, there springs up precisely in the younger generation a deep mistrust of institutions, norms, and regulations. The Church with her hierarchical constitution, her dogmas and her norms is contrasted with the spirit of Christ. But the spirit needs vessels which can preserve it and transmit it. Christ Himself is the origin of the Church's mission and authority, in which His promise is fulfilled: "Lo, I am with you always, to the close of the age" (Mt. 28:20).

Dear brothers, keep all needs and problems of men present in your heart—and in their midst proclaim firmly what Jesus demands, without leaving out anything.... Do this because you are concerned about man. Only the man who is capable of a complete and definitive decision, the man whose body and soul are in harmony, the man who is ready to use his whole strength for his salvation, is invulnerable against the secret decomposition of the fundamental substance of humanity.

So devote special attention to youth, among whom there can be seen such promising enthusiasm, but also such estrangement from the Church! Turn with particular care and cordiality to couples and families—the Synod of Bishops, which recently concluded in Rome, must not remain mere theory, but must be filled with life. The alienation of a large part of the working-class population from the Church; the distance between intellectuals and the Church; woman's need, in such changed conditions, to be accepted and feel completely fulfilled both on the Christian and on the human plane: these indications widen the field of our common effort, in order that men may believe tomorrow as well.

I am convinced that a new impetus of moral consciousness and Christian life are closely, in fact indissolubly, linked with one condition: the revival of personal confession. Make this a priority of your pastoral care!

ATTENTION TO SPIRITUAL VOCATIONS

7. *Turn your particular attention to the future of spiritual vocations and pastoral services.*

According to human reckoning, the number of priests who are available for service in the apostolate will be reduced by a good third within a decade. I share from the bottom of my heart the concern that this gives you. I am convinced with you that it is a good thing to stimulate with might and main the service of the permanent diaconate, and also the service of the laity, which is mainly volunteer service, but also professional, for the tasks of pastoral work. The service of priests, however, cannot be replaced by other services. Your tradition of the care of souls absolutely cannot be compared with the conditions of Africa or Latin America. Yet, this makes me think that I met far greater optimism there than in Western Europe, although the number of pastors available there is far less. I consider it one of the most important tasks to do everything possible, with the commitment of prayer and of spiritual testimony, so that God's call to the young to make themselves available for complete service of the Lord may become audible, and that premises in the family, in the community, and in youth associations may grow for this purpose. But panic at the difficult situation dims our view of what the Lord wants of us. The fact that sensitivity to the evangelical counsels and to priestly celibacy is decreasing considerably represents a state of spiritual emergency just as much as the shortage of priests. Certainly, the salvation of souls is the supreme law. But precisely this salvation of souls demands that we should stir up the communities themselves, that we should encourage every baptized and confirmed person to bear witness to faith, that we should stimulate spiritual vitality in our families, our groups, our communities and our movements. Then the Lord will be able to speak and call—and we will be able to hear.

I have also mentioned the great importance of the presbyterate round the bishop. Could not the spiritual service be perceived more effectively if the bond between priests were closer? I would like to mention here once more the great importance of the spiritual community of priests, which can free individuals from excessive demands and isolation. To the extent to which you commit yourselves unanimously and clearly for common testimony to the priesthood in celibacy and for a form of life based on the spirit of the evangelical counsels, the Lord will not be sparing of His gifts of grace.

CONCERN FOR UNIVERSAL HEART AND VIEW

8. *Be concerned about a universal heart and a universal view for your faithful.*

Allow me to refer to my message for the Berlin Katholikentag: help to construct a universal "civilization of love"! I would like to call your attention in the first place to the dimension of the "universal." To be Christians and to be men today, must be to be universal, to be "catholic." Join to the commitment of your availability for material aid also the commitment of your spiritual and religious forces for all, and be ready, too, to receive and learn! There is such humanity not utilized, such spiritual experience, such witness of constructive faith in the young Churches that our Western countries, now weary, could draw new youth and new life from them.

We certainly cannot ignore a painful reality. In many parts of the world the Church is persecuted; many Christians, many people are prevented from enjoying their full rights of freedom. Do not take the freedom in your society for granted, but as a commitment for others who do not have this freedom!

Your country is in Europe. I was able to collaborate repeatedly with many of you, when I was Archbishop of Krakow, to animate Europe, to anchor its unity to its spiritual and religious foundations. Just think, Europe can renew itself and unite only from those roots which brought Europe into existence! Think finally of this, precisely in your country: Europe embraces not only the north and the south, but also the west and the east!

A piece of Europe, a piece of the world, becomes more and more present in your country through the many foreigners who are living and working among you. Here you have an urgent task, both on the ecclesial plane and on the social one. Think of Him who died for everyone and who made us all His brothers and sisters.

COMMITMENT TO HUMAN SOCIETY

9. *Commit yourselves for human rights and for the solid foundations of human society in your land.*

You live in a society in which a high degree of protection for freedom and human dignity is guaranteed. Be grateful for this but do not allow arbitrary action to be propagated, in the name of freedom, which strikes at the inviolability of the life of every man, also of unborn life. Realize, too, the dignity and the right of marriage and the family! Only respect of inalienable fundamental rights and values guarantees that freedom that does not lead to self-destruction! Think about this: the more law and morality differ, the more urgent is the juridical protection of fundamental moral convictions.

The Church in your country has an abundance of institutions for education and instruction, Caritas, and social service. Defend the ability of making your Christian contribution to the construction of society. Think also of this: credible witness grows only from internal adherence to Jesus Christ and not from a mere external agreement with other forces of society.

A LIFE IN THE SPIRIT OF CHRIST

10. *Against excessive demands and consumerism, propose the alternative of a life in the Spirit of Christ.*

On the one hand the desire for possessions and consumerism is growing, so that to have is considered far more than to be (cf. *Redemptor hominis,* no. 16). On the other hand we are reaching the limit of economic and technical growth. Do we want to build a road towards the decline and ruin of life on our earth instead of towards progress? The example of Christians is necessary. In the hope of future goods, they do not cling to fleeting ones, and therefore develop a civilization of love. So stimulate the readiness, so indispensable to be a Christian, for sacrifice and renunciation, and let us also recognize the importance of the evangelical counsels for the whole of society!

11. "God did not give us a spirit of timidity but a spirit of power and love and self-control" (2 Tm. 1:7).

Dear and venerated brothers in the episcopal office, your task is a grave one. In order that the Apostles, whose successors we are, would be able to carry it out, the Lord gave them His Holy Spirit. Let us make room in us and among us for this Spirit. His characteristics are: power, wisdom, love. Power, unconcerned about approval or resistance, to let the Lord Himself speak and operate; power, the most interior measurement of which is the weakness of the cross. Wisdom, which looks with firmness at the truth of Jesus Christ, but also listens without prejudice to the problems and concerns of modern man. Finally, and above all, love, which risks everything, endures everything and hopes for everything; love, which creates unity, because it walks with Jesus Christ to the cross, unites heaven and earth and brings together all the separated. I promise you to bear your burden with you in a brotherly way and I implore from you unshakable unity, becoming deeper and deeper, in this Spirit. May Mary, Queen of the Apostles and Mother of the Church, be with us so that a new Pentecost may be prepared.

SERVING OUR NEIGHBOR IS PROCLAIMING THE GOSPEL

On Tuesday, November 18, in the Cathedral of Fulda, the Pope met with laity professionally committed to the service of the Church, and delivered the following message.

Brothers and sisters in Christ,
Dear collaborators in the ministry of the Church,

Following my meeting with the priests and bishops at the tomb of St. Boniface, it was my special wish to meet with you here in this memorable place, since you bear such a large share of the everyday workload in fulfilling the mission of the Church. I am filled with joy at seeing that so many of you have been able to come today and I extend my cordial greetings to all of you.

1. Since the foundation of the Church of Jesus Christ, an important characteristic of His disciples has always been that they are of one heart and one

mind. In the first Christian communities there was already the simultaneous development of a wealth of ministries, gifts and duties. St. Paul repeatedly uses the image of a body with many members. These ministries are by no means limited to ordained priesthood. In the building up of congregations, in bearing witness to the faith, or in service to one's neighbor, the Church has a large number of different duties which basically any Christian can fulfill who has been baptized and confirmed, and who actively lives in the union of the Church.

Especially in the case of the young Churches, the Gospel can only grow when many dedicate themselves fully to these many services. But is not the same thing necessary on the old continent of Europe, where the Church has been increasingly immersed in a secular world? The life of the Church in your country, too, is more than ever dependent upon the many who consider the cause of the Church their own cause and invest their energies and their time so that the Church is, and will remain, full of life and credible. In this the main weight lies on the voluntary ministry carried out by countless people in addition to their normal work, and often with great sacrifices. However, it is the sign of the dynamic nature of the Church when people place all of their skills and all of their time, thus as a profession, at the Church's disposal. Many of the works and achievements in the pastoral, social and educational areas that are characteristic of the Church of your country would not be possible without full-time collaborators. It is a great pleasure for me today to meet this group, knowing that it is so important in carrying out the ministry of the Church. The large number of people in the full-time employ of the Church is a specific characteristic of your country. And I know of the pioneering effort that has been carried out by the women in this country, especially in charity and pastoral work.

I would like to take this opportunity to express my sincere gratitude and recognition to all voluntary and full-time collaborators in the ministry of the Church, through which they are effectively involved in its redemptive mission. This is meant for everyone without exception, no matter where they work, even though I may not be able to mention expressly every individual group in what follows, for lack of time.

To have a Church-related occupation as a layman often means dedication to the Church in opposition to normal living habits, and the need to harmonize the requirements of a Church-related occupation with the requirements of one's family and those of one's personal life. You will only be able to do this through living more consciously from the source of life, from the Holy Spirit, whom you received at Baptism and at your Confirmation. I would like to encourage you in this and give you a few indications as to how you can understand and carry out your important ministry in this Spirit. The Lord said to Peter, "Strengthen your brothers," and that I feel to be my mission towards you. What does strengthening you imply? This means encouraging you to live in the Spirit that filled Jesus Christ who leads the Church and qualifies it for the mission that each of you receives at Baptism and Confirmation and which is a source of strength for your ministry. It is the spirit of *love*, the spirit of *witnessed faith*, the spirit of the *children of God*, and the spirit of *unity*.

LOVE—THE CHARISM
THAT SURPASSES ALL

2. Paul writes in his Epistle to the Romans: "The love of God is placed in our hearts by the Holy Spirit" (15:30). The Spirit of God first manifests itself as *love*. Love is at the same time the fruit of the Spirit and is thus an indication that it is at work. Love is the highest of the gifts of grace, the charism that surpasses all others.

The Church has been called to preach and to teach this love, which in the end is God Himself, to men through word and deed. The Church can only carry out its ministry if a little of the redemptive content of its message becomes tangibly manifest in this world. Thus, from the outset the preaching of the Word has been accompanied by the act of love, whether in the case of the Lord Himself, who healed the sick and cared for the starving in the wilderness, or in the time of the modern Church, where we have the example of special care for the poor in Jerusalem, or compensation between rich and poor congregations. Deaconship in all its forms is an indispensable part of the work of proclaiming the Gospel. This kind of deaconship determines the basic attitude of all ministries in the Church. Love is simultaneously the foundation and the completion, the beginning and the end of every calling, every gift of grace and every Christian duty.

In this context I would like to say a few words to those of you who work in the field of charity for the Church. Charity work has had an important history in your country since the foundation of the German Charity Association by Lorenz Werthmann. The tree that he planted at the end of the last century has truly borne rich fruit. The members of your association come from all sections and sectors of the society of the Federal Republic. They stand in the service of young and old, children and families, the handicapped and the sick. Involving nearly 300,000 men and women, the charity services represent a whole army of helpers, truly a supporting column in the social sphere of the Federal Republic of Germany.

Actually, I do not need to emphasize that your effort is a source of great joy to me. First of all, simply because you do so much good; because you wipe away tears and feed the hungry; because you comfort the lonely, soothe pain and make recovery from illness possible. But also because your ministry proves that "all paths of the Church lead to man" (*Redemptor hominis,* no. 14).

The fact that even so-called godless or areligious groups in our societies seek to experience the goodness and the benevolence of God in the Church is evidence of an instinctive knowledge of God's goodness and the association of the Church with God's message. For you who carry out charity work for the Church, this means, of course, responsibilities that can hardly be overestimated. You stand like a column in the stream of our changing society, in which there is an increasing threat to human dignity, to the dignity of unborn life, that of old people, those with incurable diseases, and also a threat to man's ability to pass life on to future generations. The protection of all these values has been largely entrusted to your hands. For many, the credibility of the Church, in which they wish to find the serving love of Christ, depends upon your service.

TECHNICAL DEVICES
CANNOT REPLACE HUMANITY

Indeed, your work must be orientated towards this need. A number of consequences derive automatically from this, but I can only refer to them briefly here. Helping one's fellowman requires thorough expert knowledge, qualified training, and employment of the best personnel and equipment. Human beings, on the other hand, need much more than just technical perfection. People have hearts and want to be cared for by people with hearts. Humanity cannot be replaced by technical devices and administration. This is another reason why, despite the requirement for expertise and instruments of the highest quality, the volunteer collaborator has an irreplaceable function in charity work. Of course he needs to be trained. But the important thing is his readiness to be of assistance to others, his ability to perceive need in others, the patience with which he is able to listen to others, his care for others without making a routine matter of it. These are all things that are not a result of his acquired *skills,* but rather are a part of *himself.*

No one should have any illusions about it. Helping one's fellowman can also become a pure routine. How poor the person in this work is, who regards his occupation merely as a means of making a living with sufficient income and regular working hours, and for whom love for his fellowman and the Gospel are unable to sustain in times of fatigue. But even for the person whose intention it might have been to consume himself in doing good by serving others, who wanted to serve the Church because acceptance of the message of Jesus is connected with the credibility of the Church, even for this person the moment will arrive when the feeling of everyday routine sets in. The ability to sympathize fades, generosity is used up, the heart is disappointed. Where does he get the strength to endure in this work? At first he notices that the demands of this work go beyond his own energies. He remembers the source from which love can be derived. Would God deny him the strength of His Spirit if he asked Him for it?

Since it is the Holy Spirit who pours God's love into our hearts, it could only be considered presumptuous of someone, whose work involves a service to his fellowman, to renounce this Spirit, since he would be content only with the love produced in his own heart. Did not all those who are considered examples of active love to one's fellowman receive their gift from the Holy Spirit? Many of them initiated movements or founded Church communities. For a period of time it was a natural fact that the spirit of the founders was passed on in them. This was easier since it mostly involved orders which, as a result of their structure, are more easily able to retain their spiritual heritage than other institutions. Today, some 30,000 of the fulltime collaborators in charity work are members of our religious orders. And no one should say that the members of these orders can be done without. The mere fact that they are there points out the interconnection of service to one's fellowman and God's making this ministry possible. No one can do without those from whom we expect help for that which is most urgently necessary, for the constant renewal and strengthening of our own ability to love through the love that God holds ready for us in His Holy Spirit.

TO RELIGION TEACHERS
AND CATECHISTS

3. The spirit that Christ places in our hearts is the spirit of *witnessed faith*. It is only in the Holy Spirit that we can witness that "Jesus is the Lord" (1 Cor. 12:3). All Christians are given the ability and called to witness their faith, and particularly those who, not only in private but also in professional life, are "people of the Church." Every one of us must ask himself whether the testimony of his personal life and his public and professional behavior corresponds to what people expect of the Church and what the Church expects of people. For many of you, witnessing of faith is directly connected with your work. In this connection I would like to direct a few words to the teachers of religion and the catechists' among you. Viewed superficially, many people today seem to be satisfied with a purely objective accomplishment, merely with what can be considered acceptably executed service. However, if one gazes more deeply into the human soul, one often sees great personal insecurity, a longing to be understood and to discover meaning in life. Many people, especially young adults, are involved in the attempt to find themselves.

They are unable to, unless someone shows them the way, unless they, especially when they are still young, are led to discover the truth about man, the truth about the world and everything it involves. Those of you who are in the employ of the Church teaching religion at schools and similar institutions are involved in making a contribution that can hardly be overestimated in its importance. You are in the position to do this because your Church has thus far been able to maintain the tradition of religious instruction at schools through the pursuit of prudent and emphatic policy in dealing with state and society. What a chance the young people of your nation have for salvation! What an opportunity there is in your country to know the Gospel! This is an opportunity that is the envy of many a non-German teacher and priest. May you be successful in making good use of this opportunity with the help of God.

This requires that you have a high degree of expertise, that you be qualified in leadership and have a solid knowledge of theology. Because of this nature of the faith, it creates a desire to be understood *(fides quaerens intellectum:* "faith seeking understanding"). In a certain sense the content of faith is like a material that takes up the energies of incessant research and yet withstands it. The matter of faith, as in many other cases—indeed, obviously more than in many other cases—attracts the questioning mind and constantly offers opportunities to test the sharpened intellect. I understand only too well that so many of you have turned completely to theology, that in your country so many laymen are dedicated to this discipline. The study of theology also has its fascinations in terms of pure knowledge. What more moving, more worthwhile object could there be for the curiosity of our minds than the Word, the Word of God and finally He Himself who communicated the Word to us?

To be sure, the content of the Word is too significant for the result of such intellectual searching to be unimportant. The question as to what decides the meaning of human life cannot be answered with either a "yes" or a "no." Here, if anywhere at all, the truth is required. It can be found, at least in the dimensions that are revealed to us as human beings. It can be taught to others, at least in the way that is possible for us as human beings.

STUDY OF CATHOLIC THEOLOGY

Opinions, private views, speculations are not enough for the person who reflects upon its influence on the life of the individual and who feels respect for the individual. And they cannot be satisfying at all to the person who has become aware that with theological answers he has reached the primal depths of truth itself. God has revealed His Word to us, which we would have been unable to find and understand merely on the strength of our intellect, no matter how much our reason is given to want to elucidate the credibility of the Word and its correlation to our human questions and knowledge. It lies in the nature of revelation that a special intellectual gift is required to preserve and interpret God's Word. Thus, the study of Catholic theology must be accompanied by the willingness to listen to the binding testimony of the Church and to accept the decision of those who, as the leaders of the Church, are responsible before God for maintaining the Faith. In a letter I wrote to the members of the German Bishops' Conference on May 15th this year, I said "the examination, recognition or rejection of a doctrine is part of the prophetic mission of the Church." Without the Church the Word of God would not have been passed down and preserved over the generations. One cannot want to have the Word of God without the Church.

Another aspect needs to be added to the intellectual understanding of faith. More than just being known, faith needs to be lived. In the New Testament a belief that culminated in pure knowledge was rejected as a perversion. In the Epistle of St. James the Apostle it is pointed out that even the powers hostile to God know of the one God; yet since their nature does not affirm this knowledge, all that is left for them to do is to tremble before God. They will receive punishment and not salvation (cf. Jas. 2:19).

When God speaks to us He does not provide us with data on things or other people. He does not communicate "something" to us, but rather Himself. Jesus is the Word, unsurpassably fraught with significance, of God communicating Himself to us, and at the same time God Himself. Thus, God's Word requires a response that must be given by the person as a whole. God's reality escapes him who restricts himself to regarding God's Word and His truth only as a neutral object of study. The suitable approach to God as God is, can only be, adoration. Master Eckehart, one of the great mystics of your people, for this reason asked his listeners "to rid themselves of God as something thought." God, if He remains a mere "He," leaves us abandoned and empty. God addresses us directly. We will only find Him if we address Him directly as well. Thus, one should, as Eckehart said, have God present "in our feelings, in our aspirations and in love." Only the person who is completely filled with an inner spiritual turning towards God as someone *present* is showing the appropriate response according to Eckehart. Jesus also requires the same directing towards Him of the person as a whole when He speaks of the message of His Father. His Word cannot be understood as the conveyance of mere objective information, but rather as a call to follow Him.

His preaching is aimed at the testimony which was clearest in the devoted lives of the first disciples. Beyond the sharing of knowledge, His message requires a personal commitment to Him, or, as is said in the Apostolic Exhortation *Catechesi tradendae*, "the communion in life with Jesus Christ" (no. 5).

Thus, your testimony, too, dear collaborators in our Church, is indispensable for the teaching of the Gospel of Jesus. *"Verba docent, exempla trahunt"* ("words teach, examples draw") was something the ancient Romans already knew.

I recently read in an episcopal letter written by African bishops that "children learn more by watching than by listening." Giving testimony is the most important service that you as teachers of religion can provide for your students: so that they will experience a little of the friendship of the Lord in their contact with you; so that reverence for God and commitment to the Church are recognizable in their behavior; so that you teach them esteem of prayer and the celebration of the Eucharist not only with words, but rather also through the testimony of your personal life.

CHURCH ADMINISTRATION AND PASTORAL WORK

4. The spirit instilled in us by the Son of God makes us sons and daughters of God. God did not place in us the spirit of slavery, but rather the spirit of sonship (cf. Rom. 8:15; Gal. 4:6). One should be able to see it in us; it should radiate from our ministry. The Church should be described by us as something inviting and attractive, as the family of God. This of course requires of us that we do not assume a servile

attitude, and do not merely make accusations and pass judgments. And at the same time it challenges those responsible in the Church to take into account this "new kind" of Gospel in their relations with those collaborating in Church work.

I am thinking here in particular of two groups involved in service to the Church, i.e., those of you working in *Church administration* and who consequently play an important part in determining the external image of the Church in your behavior towards the general public, and then the large number of those who are directly involved in *pastoral work,* serving the family of God in the parishes and in pastoral duties.

It is to you, our dear collaborators in the pastoral area, that I want to address myself now. There are only very few of you compared with the number of full-time employees in other areas of Church work. However, your service has a special place among all the services rendered by lay members of the Church. You assist in building up the parishes, in giving testimony of the Gospel in the different parish groups and situations that life involves, in leading those who stand afar back to the Church, and in the training of voluntary assistants.

CHOICE OF PATH
NOT WITHOUT HARDSHIPS

The surge of commitment among laymen to serve the welfare of their fellowman belies all pessimism. One need only look at the number of young people who are willing to render this service. No one who takes this into consideration should maintain that the

Gospel has lost any of its attractiveness. Everyone who goes into the ministry of the Church has his own history behind him. It is unlikely that any of you chose this path to the acclaim of surrounding opinion. Rather, it is more likely that it was done accompanied by the critical comments of classmates or perhaps even members of your families. In the opinion of many people, one cannot make one's willingness to devote one's life to helping other people into one's occupation. This, it is said, is absolutely old-fashioned. And if, in addition to this, the future contours of the ministry are not quite clear, in some cases unpredictable, the choice of this path, in the eyes of many, borders on the unreasonable.

But you realized that the Word of God and the mission of the Church require people to help in their fulfillment, and that you must not evade this necessity. And I am sure that by now you have not only felt the burden of such responsibilities, but have already been shown gratitude by many people. Such gratitude is, however, the best confirmation of the meaningfulness of our work.

We must remember this even if a further clarification of your professional situation makes a number of considerations necessary, or if you do not experience the acceptance and approval in your parishes that you had hoped to find. It seems important to me, especially in hardship situations, that you proceed with prudence and remember the idealism with which you began, and that you try to gradually convince your co-workers and the members of the parish. We all believe that the same Spirit who gives guidance to the parishes and the hearts of men, created your ministry in the Church. Precisely in moments of affliction you are called upon to give yourself over to this Spirit.

I know that my advice to you represents a considerable demand. It implies that someone should not let himself be affected by the constant calculation of the number of hours worked and one's right to leisure time, although this sort of thing is seen in the newspapers every day; it implies that he should leave behind him the tendency to think in terms of promotions, although this is common practice in our society; it implies that in this way he should be more and more successful in identifying, not with the Church free of sin that we all dream of, but rather with the physical Church of today that does not cease to be affected by human weakness.

This kind of identification by no means makes us blind, but rather it makes us see in the correct manner, that is, the good that one discovers only with the heart, i.e., with a look of benevolence. In this way it is possible to find and convincingly pass on what is positive. One can attempt to understand the decisions of those who bear responsibility for the Church, namely, bishops and priests, even though others criticize them. Skepticism or the cultivation of inner aloofness is not what is needed, but rather confidence.

And one last thing: In the pastoral area there is also the office of the *permanent deacon,* who, following God's call, opens his heart to the sacramental gift of grace, in order to be close to people, helping them and giving testimony from the altar, the spiritual center of the Church. Liturgy and preaching, the pastoral function and deaconship here demonstrate their intimate connection. If you feel that God has called you for this, please accept your calling.

SPIRIT OF ONENESS

5. The Spirit you have received is, after all, the Spirit of *oneness*. The many ministries are a manifestation and a gift of the one Spirit. Everyone must have the courage to affirm a special gift and duty. However, this means that at the same time I must take the faith and mission of my fellowman as seriously and esteem it as much as I do my own. Working together, being considerate to one another, showing constant willingness for reconciliation and a new beginning together, is just as important as being faithful to one's own mission. Unity means, after all, open, good, patient, understanding cooperation among priests, deacons and laymen. Testimony of this unity will be possible only if everyone makes an effort to attain it "so that the world will believe" (Jn. 17:21).

At this point I would like to add a very special request. Make the concern of the Church for vocations to the priesthood and to our religious orders your own concern!

You may all be sure of my support of your service to the Church. I ask you to support mine as well. Then the Spirit of the Lord will renew the face of the Church and that of the earth through us.

"THE LOVE OF CHRIST IS STRONGER!"

On November 18, the fourth day of his pilgrimage in Germany, the Pope met with the Central Committee of German Catholics in the seminary in Fulda, near the Cathedral. The Holy Father delivered the following address.

Ladies and gentlemen,
Dear brothers and sisters,

Mr. President, please let me first of all thank you for the friendly welcome. In the course of my stay in Germany it is a great pleasure for me to be here with you and the members of the Central Committee. As you know I, as Archbishop of Krakow, for many years was chairman of the Commission of the Polish Bishops' Conference for matters concerning the laity. On the Krakow Diocesan Synod, too, the cooperation with the laity was of special importance to me. From such experience I know about the importance of the layman's contribution to the shaping of Church life and to the testimony of the Christian message in the world. By founding many Catholic organizations in the crucial tests of the struggles between Church and state during the last century, by means of the Central

Committee of German Catholics, by means of the hitherto eighty-six meetings of German Catholics, the German lay apostolate has gotten its unmistakable characteristics. Therefore, I am glad to be able to look at the living presence of this history, now gathered here before me: the representatives of the Central Committee, the representatives of the associations and of the diocesan councils of Catholics. And what finally completes the circle is the representation of the meeting of German Protestants which for a long time has already closely cooperated with the Central Committee and the meetings of Catholics.

Mr. President, you have referred to my message sent to the 86th Meeting of German Catholics in Berlin. This meeting and its slogan can also serve as a starting point for my short answer to your friendly welcoming words. "The love of Christ is stronger!" I think one could sum up under this sentence the experience of a more than one-hundred-year-old history of a strong and united lay apostolate in your country. The love of Christ was stronger than all secularistic tendencies in politics and culture; they neither could weaken nor disintegrate the vital energy and social creative power of the Catholic Church in Germany. The love of Christ also proved stronger than everything in the history of your country which could have pulled apart Pope and bishops on the one side, and Catholic laymen on the other. The reconstruction work in your country after the war cannot be imagined without the great contribution of German Catholicism. The work of Catholic laymen in the fields of culture, education, social commitment, and politics not only is a part of Church history, but also a part of national and European history. Where does the energy for such a work come from? Furthermore, where does the energy come from which has contributed to numerous and important steps of reconciliation between Germany and its Eastern and Western neighbors? For Christians, there is only one answer; they answer with the slogan of the Meeting of German Catholics, saying that the love of Christ is stronger.

THE CHALLENGE
OF TODAY'S MANIFOLD PROBLEMS

You certainly have not chosen this slogan in order to express your own experience formed in the past. As it is our duty, you have looked to the future, you have looked at the tasks with which all of us will have to deal in the years to come. The fields of duties which you mentioned in your report given to me are a challenge to give room to the stronger love of Christ, that is, to humbly, resolutely, and doggedly look for solutions resulting from this love, even for those problems which very often can be hardly solved by man. It is just believing in the fact that the love of Christ is stronger that can give us the unabashed strength to stand up against indifference, resignation, helplessness, fear of life, and cynicism, and for the unshortened message of the Gospel. At those places where we act like that, where we clearly and directly preach the Gospel and underline it by our way of living, people will listen very attentively. This applies to young people in particular. We have to create living cells in which believing people pass on and exemplify through their own life how relieving it is to be in the imitation of Christ. This won't, however, solve all our problems at once, but it would let the courage grow to start out to work against every weariness of norms, institutions and traditions, and instead to commit oneself to Church, its community, its example and its message, and also to its ministry and its pastorate.

You are right when concentrating your work on the various fields of politics and society, the living together of peoples, and on the world of labor and economy. Your attention is directed to today's problems of marriage and family, the social service, but also to the arts and the world of media. For the solutions of those problems left open, you try to find an appropriate judgment and bases of Christian action in the Gospel and in the Christian social doctrine. That is exactly what the Second Vatican Council, by means of the world mission of laymen, in a special way wanted to put forward again and worldwide. Do not diminish your efforts in this field and do not confine yourself to what has been already achieved. If, in this world, the Gospel shall be the leaven which penetrates the flour of earthly reality; if here too, the love of Christ shall prove stronger, it requires the openness to new horizons, it requires the understanding of new developments and situations. How about the presence of Christianity in your country—to mention a few examples only—in modern literature, theater and arts? How about the presence of Church and Christians in the sphere of press, radio and television? Does there exist a convincing Christian contribution of the hitherto unusual living together of foreigners and Germans in your big cities, in your companies? How about the matter-of-factness for you concerning the fellowship of the various peoples and cultures in the one world? How serious is your commitment for the pressing questions of energy and environment? I know that you do not ignore all these problems and I thank you for that. But at the same time I would like to encourage you to enter with resolution upon new ways, which will make many people in your country and beyond the borders of your country join unanimously in the confession of Berlin: Yes, the love of Christ really is stronger!

CO-RESPONSIBLE
FOR THE CHURCH'S
FUTURE

On Tuesday, November 18, at the Mass celebrated in the square of the cathedral, the Holy Father concluded his visit to Fulda. The large congregation was composed mostly of members of lay associations. The Pope delivered the following homily.

1. Permit me, esteemed brothers in episcopal and sacerdotal ministry, brothers and sisters of the religious orders and congregations; permit me, those representatives of the lay apostolate here today, first of all to pay my respects to the man whose tomb we have come to visit on our pilgrimage to Fulda, the shrine of your nation.

St. Boniface was a Benedictine monk, a member of that venerable order which had come to the British Isles with the monk Augustine at the time of Gregory the Great. Boniface heard the call of the peoples who inhabited Germania, the regions east of the Rhine. He followed it as the call of Christ and thus set foot on the land of your ancestors.

St. Boniface, bishop and martyr, means the "beginning" of the Gospel and of the Church in your country. We have come here today to follow on from that beginning, in order to open up his dimensions for ourselves. The "beginning" means the work of God Himself who used the testimony of man for His purpose: the testimony of Boniface, of his life and his martyrdom.

2. In the Second Reading St. Paul addresses us in the words of his Epistle to the Thessalonians, but no one doubts that the words of the Apostle of the Gentiles can also be put in the mouth of the Apostle of Germany. They spring from his heart as they once sprang from the heart of Paul of Tarsus.

"We had courage in our God to declare to you the Gospel of God in the face of great opposition" (1 Thes. 2:2). To you? Who were those peoples? What were the historical names of those tribes to whom Boniface came as a missionary? The historians referred to the Turingians, the Hessians, the Alemanni, the Bavarians, and the Friesians. St. Boniface, at whose tomb we stand here today in Fulda, brought to these peoples the message of the Gospel and that unprecedented love which, through the strength of the Holy Spirit, has become the legacy of his heart—for him as for many before and after him: for apostles, missionaries and shepherds. "We came to you as apostles of Christ," writes Paul: "We were gentle among you, like a nurse taking care of her children. So, desirous of you, we were ready to share with you not only the Gospel of God but also our own selves, because you had become most dear to us" (1 Thes. 2:7-8).

BUILT ON TRUTH AND LOVE

3. Let us now turn away from the lesson of the Epistle to the Thessalonians and imagine ourselves in the room of the Last Supper on the Thursday before Easter. Christ says: "No longer do I call you servants, for the servant does not know what his master is doing. But I have called you friends, for all that I have heard from my Father I have made known to you" (Jn. 15:15). A significant contrast: a servant is the one who does not know; a friend, the one who has been told everything, the one who knows.

And what does this friend and apostle know? He knows what Christ Himself has heard from the Father. Because Christ has told precisely everything He has learned from the Father to those who are His chosen ones: the Apostles, the friends.

Boniface, who came to the land of your ancestors centuries ago, had the same awareness and the same certainty which Christ gave to His Apostles at the Last Supper when He called them friends. We preach "as we have been approved by God to be entrusted with the Gospel, so we speak, not to please men but to please God, who tests our hearts" (1 Thes. 2:4). These words were written by Paul, the Apostle of the Gentiles, but today's liturgy places them in the mouth of Boniface, the Apostle of Germany. And it does so with every right. The work of evangelization which he carried out in your country is based on the fact that he proclaimed God's teaching—and only God's teaching. He was prepared to sacrifice his life out of love for those to whom he had been sent. The Gospel and the Church are built on the foundation of divine truth and of the love which "was poured forth into our hearts by the Holy Spirit" (Rom. 5:5).

THE STAMP OF THE CROSS

4. But the people do not always like the Gospel. Nor can it always be pleasing to them. It must not be falsified to become "flattering compliments," nor should one seek personal advantage in it, nor "conceited glory." Some who listen to it might consider it "tough speech," and those who preach and believe in it can become a "sign of contradiction." For this divine truth, this Word of God, does indeed contain considerable tension. It is the contrast between that which comes from God and that which comes from the world. Christ says: "If you were of the world, the world would love you as its own. But because you are not of the world...the world hates you" (Jn. 15:19). And "know that it has hated me before you" (Jn. 15:18).

The heart of the Gospel, the Word of the Lord, bears the stamp of the cross. In it the two great currents overlap: one, which flows from God to the world, to the people in the world, a flow of love and truth; the second, which flows through the world: the concupiscence of the eyes, the concupiscence of the flesh, and the pride of life (1 Jn. 2:16). They are not "of the Father."

This intersection of two currents continues and repeats itself in the course of history in different ways. At its center Christ Himself lives on. Christ did not come into the world merely to condemn it from the high seat of judgment of absolute transcendental truth. He came so that the world would be redeemed through Him. And that is why He sends His disciples into the world, into "the whole world." He says to them: "If they have persecuted me they will also persecute you. If they have kept my word they will keep yours also" (Jn. 15:20). Must we not, here at the tomb of St. Boniface in Fulda, ponder the wonderful expressiveness of these words?

GERMANY'S FIRST PATRON SAINT

5. We have considered all the implications of today's Gospel and lessons; we have meditated upon them with great care in order to honor Germany's first patron saint, because all words of the liturgy relate to him. They speak of him. He has therefore become a kind of cornerstone of the Church in your country because these words have attained fulfillment in him.

Just as yeast permeates flour, Boniface has with his testimony permeated and transformed the hearts of people in the spirit of Christ. In commemorating him we pay tribute to all the sons and daughters of your homeland, just as the First Reading from the Book of Ecclesiasticus speaks of them: "Let us now praise famous men, and our fathers in their generations. The Lord apportioned to them great glory, his majesty from the beginning. There were those who ruled in their kingdoms, and were men renowned for their power, giving counsel by their understanding, and proclaiming prophecies. All these were honored in their generations, and were the glory of their times. There are some of them who have left a name, so that men declare their praise. But these were men of mercy, whose righteous deeds have not been forgotten; their posterity will remain with their descendants, and their inheritance to their children's children" (Eccl. 44:1-3, 7-8, 10-11).

How many names and family names ought one to mention here! Here are just a few examples: Bruno von Querfurth and Benno von Meissen; Hildegard von Bingen and Elisabeth von Thüringen; Hedwig von Andechs and Gertrud von Helfta; Albert the Great and Peter Canisius; Edith Stein and Alfred Delp, Franz Stock and Karl Sonneschein. Truly "these were men of mercy whose righteous deeds have not been forgotten..." (Eccl. 44:10). "Their bodies were buried in peace, and their name lives to all generations. People will declare their wisdom and the congregation proclaim their praise" (Eccl. 44:14-15).

SHARING THE MISSION
OF ST. BONIFACE

6. And behold, by following the trend of thought of this lesson from the Old Testament and turning our eyes to this wonderful picture, we come to your generation in the present.

Dear brothers and sisters, our situation, our responsibility, in spite of all the differences, does indeed have much in common with the mission of Saint Boniface. With him began the history of Christianity in your country. Many say that that evolution is drawing to an end. I say to you: this history of Christianity in your country should now experience a new beginning through you, through your testimony shaped in the spirit of St. Peter!

How wonderful it is that I am able to impress this upon you, dear Catholics from the councils and associations of the lay apostolate. The history of the Catholic associations over the past 130 years, but also the activities of the councils of the lay apostolate who have a good position in this country and have arisen everywhere since the Second Vatican Council, are a promising basis for the fulfillment of the mission of the hour. Do not rest on your oars, but courageously venture a new beginning like Boniface. Give as "friends of Christ" the "Gospel of God" and your "own soul"! (Jn. 15:15; 1 Thes. 2:8)

GIVING WOMEN SIGNIFICANCE AND RESPECT

7. Not only did the faith grow through Boniface, but there blossomed that human civilization which is the fruit and the confirmation of the faith. In spreading the faith and in your world mission you too have your principal duty as lay people. If the people, especially the young, impetuously ask about the meaning of life, give them a convincing, a comprehensible answer. If the right to life, if the moral principles of true human civilization are threatened, you should protect that life and the dignity of man! If education merely presents a functionalistic, meaningless image of man, you should stand up for the kind of education that starts from man as the image of God! When consumption on the one hand and the fear of the limits of growth on the other determine the mood of society, you should develop a new lifestyle and conditions of life which testify to the hope which Christ gives us.

The sister of St. Boniface was a great woman: the abbess St. Lioba, whose tomb is venerated only a few kilometers from here; you should give the women in our society and Church the significance and respect which will enable them to fulfill their important mission for a truly human and Christian life. If, despite all progress of mankind, those groups who live on the fringe of society or do not have their fair share in the fruits of general development do not grow, you should stand up for the rights and for the happiness of all; you should be champions of a universal social order, of freedom, justice and peace.

8. Dear brothers and sisters, you share responsibility for the future of our Church. Be yourselves the Church, totally. In your associations give prominence to the essential characteristics of the Church, of the one, holy, catholic and apostolic Church.

Be as one among yourselves; be—in keeping with your great traditions—pillars and supports of unity between the flock of Christ and their shepherds sent by Christ. Let not your actions be governed by prestige, egoism, selfishness, but be "one heart and one soul" (Acts 4:32). Foster with all your energy the unity of separated Christians! The unity of the Church was the passion of St. Boniface.

Be holy! Yes, sanctify your own life and keep in your midst the one who alone is holy. Only if you make the unmistakable characteristics of the Gospel the focal point of your life will you be able to inspire and attract people. And in your world mission promote the sanctification of the world. Boniface was a saint in life and in death.

Be catholic, all-embracing, open-minded, and universal like Boniface, who linked England and Ger-

Dear brothers and sisters, you share responsibility for the future of our Church. Be yourselves the Church, totally. In your associations give prominence to the essential characteristics of the Church, of the one, holy, catholic and apostolic Church.

Be as one among yourselves; be—in keeping with your great traditions—pillars and supports of unity between the flock of Christ and their shepherds sent by Christ.

many and Rome in his life and in his heart. Do not
lock yourselves away in your own cares and problems. Your work for the whole of mankind, for the
Third World, for Europe, is needed to make a success
of the new beginning.

And finally be apostles, witnesses of the Faith
following the example of the martyr and apostle
of the Germans, Boniface, as one with Pope and bishops, but at the same time possessing the courage to
carry out his own irreplaceable mission.

9. Permit me, dear brothers and sisters, to conclude these deliberations at the tomb of St. Boniface,
the apostle of your country, with a wish which I take
from today's liturgy. We read in the Book of Sirach:
"Their descendants stand by the covenants; their
children also for their sake. Their posterity will continue forever and their glory will not be blotted out"
(44:12-13).

What more can I wish you, the present generation of Christians in Germany? And what could we together beseech more fervently here at this shrine?
That subsequent generations will preserve their faith
in the covenant. That Christ be their way, their truth,
and their life. That they, like you, may come to this
place which signifies the "beginning" of God's work
in your homeland. That from here they may shape the
present ever anew.

...and your glory shall not be forsaken.

HELP TO PERFECT
THE FREEDOM
OF THE GIFT

On Tuesday, November 18, the Holy Father celebrated Mass for religious in Altötting, a Bavarian city which has a Marian Sanctuary that is the goal of continuous pilgrimages. During the Mass in the main square of the city, the Pope delivered the following homily.

Dear brothers and sisters in the Lord,

1. On the pilgrimage through your country we come together at the House of the Lord, at this sanctuary, in order to meet in a special way *with Mary, our Blessed Lady.* You, reverend brothers and sisters who as members of religious orders, secular institutes, and other religious communities are living a special vocation, participate in this meeting most of all. You can say about yourselves that through your consecrated, total offering of yourselves "your life is hidden with Christ in God" (Col. 3:3).

Together with you I come as a pilgrim to the sanctuary of Altötting. Together with you I rejoice in the presence of Cardinal Joseph Ratzinger, the Archbishop of Munich and Freising, of Bishop Antonius Hofmann, of many bishops and auxiliaries, and of numerous pilgrims—priests and lay people—from Bavaria and the neighboring states who have gathered here for this evening Eucharistic celebration. A most cordial *Vergelt's Gott* (God bless you) for your coming!

Thank you for the prayer and the mostly secret and silent sacrifices whereby for weeks you have been spiritually preparing this meeting. Thank you for your ready fidelity to the Successor of Peter which you have shown in your welcoming address. Such loving community allows me today, the feast of the consecration of the Cathedral of St. Peter and St. Paul in Rome, to feel at home with you.

Allow me to compare our common visit in Altötting with *Mary's visit* to Zachary and Elizabeth. I am confident that our visit will bear abundant fruit if we try to make it similar to Mary's. In this we want to be guided as much as possible by the light of the Word of God which we hear in this liturgy.

2. Mary enters the house of her relative, she greets Elizabeth, and hears her words of greeting. These words are most familiar to us. We repeat them innumerable times, especially when we meditate on the mysteries of the rosary: *"Blessed are you among women,* and blessed is the fruit of your womb" (Lk. 1:42). That is how the wife of Zachary greets Mary. With these words she proclaims a first beatitude whose sound echoes in the history of the Church and of mankind, in the history of human hearts and thoughts. Has man ever been able to attain to anything more exalted? Has he ever been able to experience about himself anything more profound? Has man been able through any achievement of his being man—through his intellect, the greatness of his mind or through heroic deeds—to be lifted up to a higher state than has been given him in this "fruit of the womb" of Mary in whom the Eternal Word, the Son who is of one being with the Father, became flesh? Is the vastness of the human heart able to receive a

greater fullness of truth and love than that in which God Himself sets about to give His only Son to man? The Son of God becomes man, conceived by the Holy Spirit! Yes indeed, Mary, you are blessed more than all other women.

To her first beatitude Elizabeth adds a second one: "Blessed is she who believed that the promise made her by the Lord would be fulfilled" (Lk. 1:45). Elizabeth extols and praises the faith of Mary. With this she entered in a profound way into the unique greatness of the moment when the Virgin from Nazareth had heard the words of the annunciation. For this message had burst open all limits of human understanding in spite of the elevated tradition of the Old Testament. And behold, Mary did not only hear these words, she did not only receive them; she gave the answer which fully responded to them: "Behold, I am the handmaid of the Lord; be it done to me according to your word" (Lk. 1:38). Such an answer demanded from Mary an unconditional faith, a faith after the example of Abraham and Moses, a faith even greater than that. It is precisely this faith of Mary which Elizabeth extols.

3. My dear brothers and sisters! With regard to the mystery of the personal call of each one of you, we can repeat in a certain sense—keeping in mind the proportions, of course: "Blessed are you because you believed." The faith of Mary has shone also in you when you spoke your "fiat," your yes to the call to the special fellowship of Christ. It was only in faith that you were able to take the first steps as people called by the Lord—just as once upon a time the disciples did at the Sea of Galilee; it was in faith that you perceived the word of the One who called you; in faith

you left behind your previous *"lebensraum"* (life) with all its possibilities; in faith you started to follow the Lord, ready from now on to expect the meaning and fruitfulness of your life only from your total union with Him.

Believing in the faithfulness of the One who calls and in the power of His Spirit, you put yourselves at God's disposal through the vows of poverty, consecrated virginity, and obedience; and this not as an "obligation which can be revoked," not as "life in a monastery for a time," not as co-workers in a group which has come together for a specific task and which breaks up again at will. No, in faith you have spoken a yes which is all-inclusive and forever and which finds its expression in your way of life and even in your religious garb. In our time where people shy away from binding ties, where many would like to turn to a "life of probation," it belongs to you to testify that one can dare to enter into a definitive bond and to take a decision for God which embraces the whole life.

Your "yes," given years or decades ago, has to be ever reaffirmed to the Lord. This requires a daily listening and probing into the daily responding to His crucified—and crucifying—love. Only He is able to keep the gift of vocation alive in you. Only He is able through His Spirit to overcome the weakness experienced time and again.

Also, Mary's "yes," which she spoke in a unique decision, had to be redeemed by her over and over again, until she was standing beneath the cross where she offered her Son and became our mother. He who wanted Mary's "yes" for the cooperation in salvation, also wants your "yes." You did say it! Say it every day anew! Then it will be true for you, too: "Blessed are you because you have believed!"

4. Faith makes the status of religious become a special witness of the coming kingdom of God. Christ speaks about this kingdom in connection with the mystery of the resurrection of the body: "In the resurrection they neither marry nor are given in marriage" (Mt. 22:30). In the liturgy we celebrate today at our Blessed Lady's in Altötting, this mystery is enunciated in the Letter of St. Paul to the Corinthians: "When this perishable nature has put on imperishability, and when this mortal nature has put on immortality, then the words of Scripture will come true: Death is swallowed up in victory. Death, where is your victory? Death, where is your sting? Now the sting of death is sin, and sin gets its power from the Law. So let us thank God for giving us the victory through our Lord Jesus Christ" (1 Cor. 15:54-57).

Today these impressive words of the Apostle of the Gentiles have been read in honor of Mary. For through her assumption into heaven she has attained to the full participation in the resurrection of Christ.

The very same words, however, the Apostle addresses also to you, dear brothers and sisters; because by the great yes of your life you have chosen consecrated celibacy "for the sake of the kingdom" (Mt. 19:12). In this way you are a visible sign of the coming kingdom of God!

The heart of each one of you who have foregone fatherhood and motherhood of this earth may be filled again and again by the inestimable richness of spiritual fatherhood and motherhood which so many of your fellow-creatures are in urgent need of! You do not love less; you love more! The fact that in a very profound way you know how to care, to help, to heal, to educate, to guide, and to console is shown, last but not least, by the many and often moving letters by which the Pope is being implored not to allow sisters, priests or brothers to be withdrawn from a certain kindergarten, a school, an old folks' home or hospital, from a station for social work, or a parish.

Why is your service valued so much? It is not only because of your professional proficiency; not only because you are able, due to your choice of life, to give more time; it is in the first place because people feel that through you someone else is at work. Because to the extent you live your full surrender to the Lord, you communicate something *from Him;* and it is He for whom the human heart is longing in the last end.

It is He whom you love in all those who are entrusted to your manifold care, your prayer of intercession, your hidden sacrifices, Him you serve "in the sick and the old, the handicapped and the under-privileged whom no one else cares for..., in the children, the young adults, in school, catechesis and pastoral work. Him you serve in the most humble things as well as in the performance of tasks which sometimes require a high education" (cf. Allocution in Czestochowa, June 5, 1979). For His sake many from your communities leave their native country in order to serve the kingdom of God in the young Churches with an untiring engagement. Him you seek and find everywhere, similar to the Bride of the Song of Songs: "...I found him whom my heart loves" (Sg. 3:4). This fulfillment of life—the fact that in everything you find *Him* and in Him everything—is at the same time the best encouragement for young

Christians to respond within the Church to the call of Jesus—also to the call to a life according to the evangelical counsels. In you they can come to understand that whosoever gives himself up has found the meaning of his life (cf. Mk. 8:35).

5. Mary, to whom we have come today as pilgrims to Altötting, carries the features of that woman whom the Apocalypse describes: "A woman adorned with the sun, standing on the moon, and with twelve stars on her head for a crown" (Rev. 12:1). The woman, who stands at the end of the history of creation and salvation, corresponds evidently to the one about whom it is said in the first pages of the Bible that she "is going to crush the head of the serpent."

Between this promising beginning and the apocalyptic end Mary has brought to light a Son "who is to rule all nations with an iron scepter" (Rev. 12:5).

Her heel it is which is being persecuted by that first "serpent." She it is with whom the apocalyptic dragon makes war, for being the Mother of the redeemed, she is the image of the Church whom we likewise call mother (cf. *Lumen gentium,* no. 68).

Dear brothers and sisters! You are called in a special way to take part in this spiritual battle! You are called into this permanent conflict which our Mother Church endures and which forms in her the image of the woman, the Mother of the Messiah. You who find the very center of your vocation in the adoration of the holy God, you are also exposed to the temptation of the evil one in a special way—as it can be seen in an exemplary way in the temptation of the Lord. The war is raging between the Word of God and the device of the evil one. Between, "Tell these stones to turn into loaves!" and, "Man does not live on bread alone'' (Mt. 4:3f.). God wants us to conquer the earth (cf. Gen. 1:28) by bringing it—and ourselves—to perfection. The temptation of the evil one wants us to disfigure it and ourselves; to become enslaved by work and spoiled by our leisure time; to make endless sacrifices for our outside and wither away inside; to adorn our home and be homeless; to value having and forget being; that possessions become our ''god'' (cf. Phil. 3:19). Through your inner battle for the spirit of poverty and through this poverty which can be seen and serves as a sign, dear sisters and brothers, you help all members of the Church and of mankind to be careful stewards of this world, to possess things in such a way that they do not possess us, not to allow the sustenance of life to become the meaning of life.

"Throw yourself down,'' says the second temptation of Jesus (cf. Mt. 4:6). Throw yourself into the adventure, dare to jump into the realm of dreams, is the allurement of today; get drunk from life's horn of plenty—in the drunkenness of speed, the drunkenness of sensuality, the drunkenness of delusions, and the drunkenness of violence. God has given us a heart to experience (and enjoy) things, and much which can fill us—above all the thou. But without Him all is too little. We either seek our happiness in Him or we miss it—being chased by our pursuit of happiness, from disappointment to disappointment, up to disgust and aversion. Through your renouncement of the thou which brings fulfillment in marriage and through your special cultivation of loving openness for God, dear brothers and sisters, you help all in the Church: to give themselves without losing themselves; to turn towards each other and so to grow in God; to enjoy the things that pass in such a way that one keeps united with the eternal things at the same time, as it is said in a liturgical prayer (Seventeenth Sunday in Ordinary Time).

Even more glorious and more dangerous than world and thou, than wealth and happiness, is the "I" and its claim to self-realization. God wants man "in his own image and likeness" (cf. Gen. 1:6f.); Lucifer wants him as an anti-god—who refuses to worship God (cf. Jer. 2:20) and in return falls a prey to idols: "He showed him all the kingdoms of the world...: I will give you all these, if you fall at my feet and worship me" (Mt. 4:8f.). All creative exertion and any self-realization—in politics, in economics, in the intellectual life, and even in the Church—carries with itself the danger of vanity, of pride and even of ruthlessness. My dear religious, by your faithful struggle for the spirit of obedience and for its visible sign, obedience towards your superior, you help all the faithful and the Church herself to understand and to overcome the temptation of power; you help them to come to the perfection of freedom in the surrender of self.

Today, maybe more than ever before, the kingdom of God which "suffers violence" (cf. Mt. 11:12) needs new "warriors" in response to the temptations and demands of our time. It wants to find them in your monasteries and communities, molded and supported by the regular life. Be convinced that such generous men and women will attract new generations who follow Christ and "renew the face of the earth" (Ps. 104:30) also today as well as tomorrow!

6. During these days of my pilgrimage with you the Church commemorates three saints of your country. To them, in conclusion, I would like to

recommend your way and service in the Church. May St. Albert help you to perceive from the signs of the time the call of God and to respond to it in the spirit of your founders. May St. Gertrude implore for you the zeal and the fruit of finding God in your meditation and liturgy. May St. Elizabeth help you to have a delicate sense and unlimited openness as you turn to all who need you. Albert, Gertrude, Elizabeth—they are joined here in Altötting by the humble and cheerful porter of St. Anne's Monastery, St. Brother Konrad. We see him kneeling in his cell—before the small window which had been made especially for him so that he could always look at the altar of the church. May we, too, in our daily lives break through the walls of the visible world in order to keep our eyes always and everywhere fixed upon the Lord! Together with Mary let us now continue our visit to the sanctuary she loves so much. Let us enter together with her and let us repeat:

"My soul proclaims the greatness of the Lord, and my spirit exults in God my savior; because he has looked upon his lowly handmaid. Yes, from this day forward all generations will call me blessed, for the Almighty has done great things for me. Holy is his name, and his mercy reaches from age to age for those who fear him" (Lk. 1:46-50).

Indeed, my dear brothers and sisters! The Almighty has done "great things" for each one of you! Great things! For each one of you! Do not cease praising Him! Do not cease thanking Him! Do not cease living your total surrender, your vocation each single day anew under the protection of the Immaculate Virgin, Our Blessed Lady of Altötting!

And so the kingdom of God will be alive in you!

UNDENIABLE DIALOGUE BETWEEN THEOLOGY AND MAGISTERIUM

On Tuesday evening, November 18, the Holy Father met with German theologians in the Capuchin Convent of "Kloster San Konrad" in Altötting. The Pope delivered the following address.

Dear professors, dear brothers,

It is a special pleasure for me to meet you here this evening. It was my personal wish to see theologians of your country, for theological science is today especially one of the most important expressions and tasks of ecclesiastical life. I most cordially greet you, and in you all theologians. You are following a great tradition as manifest in the works of St. Albert the Great, Nikolaus von Kues, Möhler and Scheeben, Guardini and Przywara, to mention only a few. I name these distinguished theologians as representatives of many others who, both past and present, have enriched and are still enriching not only the Church in countries where German is spoken, but the theology and the life of the Church as a whole.

For this reason I wish to express my sincere thanks for this work to you and to all those you represent. Scientific study nearly always involves self-denial and quiet perseverance. This applies particularly to the task of providing reliable texts and exploring the sources of theology. Many patristic, medieval and modern text editions are the result of the selfless work of scholars from your country. The wider the range of theological knowledge, the more urgent the task of establishing a synthesis. In numerous glossaries, commentaries and handbooks, you have provided very helpful surveys on the state of developments in nearly all fields of study. Especially in the post-Conciliar period such fundamental guidance is very important. These works inform us about the legacy of the past with the insight of the present. In the field of biblical interpretation the co-operation among exegesis scholars has been very gratifying. It has also given strong impulses for ecumenical work and will no doubt give more. May I request all of you to continue this well-founded theological research. In doing so, be very exact in your consideration of the problems and cares of the people. But do not let yourselves be led astray by chance and short-lived currents of human thought. Scientific and especially theological discernment calls for courage to venture forth and the patience of maturity. It has its own laws which it should not allow to be imposed upon from outside.

One reason why theological research is one of the real treasures of the Church in your country is no doubt the fact that the faculty of theology has a place in the state universities. The relationship between the freedom of scientific theology and its link with the Church, as embodied in the concordats, has time and again proved to be a successful model in spite of some conflicts. This relationship affords you the opportunity to study philosophy and theology in the context of, and in cooperation with, all the science faculties of a modern university. This situation has also enhanced the quality of the colleges of philosophy and theology of the dioceses and orders, of the comprehensive universities and teacher-training colleges, and of the ecclesiastical research institutes. Moreover, the publication of theological findings would not be possible without efficient Catholic publishing companies. My thanks go to all those who in their various ways help to foster the science of theology.

Those with exceptional intellectual gifts also have great responsibility, especially in the present situation which at times appears critical. I wish, therefore, to take this opportunity to draw your attention to three perspectives which I deem particularly important.

FOSTER ANEW THE UNDERSTANDING OF GOD

1. The complexity and specialization of today have produced an abundance of tasks and queries, methods and disciplines. They have produced valuable findings and new appraisals. But there is a danger of the sheer quantity in any one branch of learning blurring the meaning and purpose of theology from time to time. As God's tracks have in any case been largely covered up in this secularized world, the concentration on the divine Trinity as the origin and lasting foundation of our life and of the whole world is the foremost task of theology today. All the passion of theological perception must ultimately lead to God Himself. As late as during the Second Vatican Council it was still believed that the

answer to the question of God's existence could be taken for granted. In the meantime, it has been seen that the very relationship between man and God has become shaky and needs to be strengthened. May I, therefore, ask you to work with all your strength to foster anew the understanding of God, and here I would emphasize the Trinity of God and the concept of creation.

This concentration on God and the salvation He brings for mankind implies an inner system of theological truths. God the Father, Jesus Christ, and the Holy Spirit are the fulcrum of that system. The Scriptures, the Church and the sacraments remain the great historical institutions of the salvation of the world. But the "hierarchy of truths" demanded by the Second Vatican Council (Decree on Ecumenism, no. 11) does not imply a simple reduction of comprehensive Catholic faith to a few basic truths, as some people thought. The more deeply and the more radically we grasp the center of things, the more distinct and the more convincing are also the lines of communication from the divine center of things to those truths which appear to be on the periphery. The depth of that concentration also reveals itself in the fact that it extends to all branches of theology. The theologian's work in the service of teaching about God is, in the view of St. Thomas Aquinas, at the same time an act of love towards man (cf. *Summ. Theol.*, II-II, qq. 181, a. 3c; 182, a. 2c; I, q. 1, a. 7c). By making him as deeply and as abundantly aware as possible that he is the thou of all divine utterances and is the object of all divine action, it explains and illustrates to him his own ultimate and eternal dimension which transcends all finite limits.

2. Every theology is based on Holy Scripture. All theological traditions derive from Holy Scripture and lead back to it. Remain, therefore, faithful to the twofold task entailed in any interpretation of Scripture. Preserve the incomparable Gospel of God which was not made by man, and at the same time have the courage to carry it out again into the world in this purity. The study of the whole Scripture therefore remains, as the Constitution on Divine Revelation of the Second Vatican Council says, "the soul of theology" (no. 24). It nourishes and rejuvenates our theological searching ever anew. Let us live our lives from the Scripture; then, whatever differences may remain, we shall still come closer to our separated brethren.

The Catholic theologian cannot build a bridge between the Scripture and the problems of the present without the mediation of Tradition. That Tradition is not a substitute for the Word of God in the Bible; rather, it testifies to it through the ages and new interpretations. Maintain your dialogue with the living Tradition of the Church. Learn from its treasures, many of which are still undiscovered. Show the people of the Church that in this process you do not rely on the relics of the past, but that our great legacy from the Apostles down to the present day is a huge reservoir from which to draw the answers to some of the questions as to the meaning of life today. We shall be better able to pass on the Word of God if we heed the Holy Scripture and its response in the living Tradition of the Church. We shall also become more critical of and sensitive to our own present. It is not the sole nor the ultimate measure of theological perception.

Explaining the great Tradition of our faith is not easy. To be able to open it up we need foreign languages, the knowledge of which is today unfortunately declining in many respects. It is essential not only to open up the sources historically, but to allow them to address us in our age. The Catholic Church, which embraces all ages of civilization, is convinced that every epoch has acquired some knowledge of the truth which is of value to us as well. Theology includes prophetic renewal from these sources, which at the same time imply an awakening and continuity. Have the courage to lead the young people, your students of philosophy and theology, to these treasures of our faith.

FAITH AS THE BASIS

3. Theology is a science with all possibilities of human perception. It is free in the application of methods and analyses. Nevertheless, theologians must see where they stand in relation to the faith of the Church. The credit for our faith goes not to ourselves; indeed, it is "built upon the foundation of the Apostles and prophets, Jesus Christ himself being the chief cornerstone" (Eph. 2:20). Theologians, too, must take faith as the basis. They can throw light on it and promote it, but they cannot produce it. They, too, have always stood on the shoulders of the fathers in the faith. They know that their specialized field does not consist of purely historical objects in an artificial test-tube, but that it is a question of the faith of the Church as experienced in life. The theologian, therefore, teaches not least in the name and on behalf of the religious community. He should and must make new proposals to contribute to the understanding of

the faith, but they are only an offer to the whole Church. Much of what he says must be corrected and expanded in a fraternal dialogue until the Church as a whole can accept it. Theology is very much a selfless service for the community of the faithful. That is why objective disputation, fraternal dialogue, openness and the willingness to modify one's own views, are essential elements of it.

THE RIGHT TO KNOW

The believer has a right to know what he can rely on in practicing his faith. Theologians must show him the means of final support. For this reason in particular the Church has been blessed with the Spirit of Truth. The sole object of teaching is to determine the truth of the Word of God, especially where there is a danger of distortion and misunderstanding. The infallibility of the Church's Magisterium must also be seen in this context. I should like to repeat what I wrote on May 15th in my letter to the members of the German Bishops' Conference: ''The Church must...be very humble and certain that it remains within that very truth, that very doctrine of faith and morals, which it has received from Jesus Christ, who has bestowed upon it in this field the gift of a special 'infallibility.' '' It is true that infallibility is not of such central importance in the hierarchy of truths, but it is ''to some extent the key to that certainty with which the faith becomes known and is preached, and also to the life and conduct of the faithful. For if one shakes or destroys that essential foundation, the most elementary truths of our faith also begin to disintegrate.''

TWO DIFFERENT TASKS

Love for the physical Church, which also includes belief in the testimony of faith and the Magisterium of the Church, does not estrange the theologian from his work and does not deprive that work of any of its indispensable self-reliance. The Magisterium and theology have two different tasks to perform. That is why neither can be reduced to the other. Yet they serve the one whole. But precisely on account of this configuration they must remain in consultation with one another. In the years since the Council you have furnished many examples of good cooperation between theology and the Magisterium. Let us deepen this basis. And whenever conflicts arise, apply your common efforts in the spirit of the common faith, of the same hope, and of the love that forms the bond between all of them.

I wanted to meet you this evening in order to confirm you in your work so far and to encourage you to pursue further achievements. Do not forget your great mission for the Church of our time. Work with care and untiringly. And while being meticulous, let your research have not only reason but also feeling. It was St. Albert the Great in particular, the 700th anniversary of whose death brought me to Germany, who constantly pointed to the need to bring science and piety, intellectual judgment and the whole individual, into harmony. Be also models of practicing faith for the many students of theology in your country, precisely at this time. Be inventive in faith so that all of us together can bring Christ and His Church nearer again, with a new language, to the many people who no longer participate in the life of the

Church. Never forget your responsibility for all members of the Church, and remember in particular the important task of teaching the faith which falls to missionaries all over the world.

Before I meet each one of you personally, please accept my fraternal greetings and God's blessing for all your colleagues, associates, and students. ''The grace of our Lord Jesus Christ and the love of God and the fellowship of the Holy Spirit be with you all'' (2 Cor. 13:13).

CHRIST ACCOMPANIES MAN IN MATURING TO HUMANITY

The first event on the Pope's last day of his pilgrimage in Germany, Wednesday, November 19, was a Mass for youth celebrated in Munich's "Theresienwiese." The Holy Father delivered the following homily.

Dear brothers and sisters,
Dear young people,

1. When Christ speaks about the kingdom of God, He often uses images and parables. His image of the "harvest," of the "great harvest," necessarily reminded His listeners of that annually recurring and so very much longed-for time when people could finally begin to harvest the fruit that had grown at the cost of considerable human effort.

The parable of the "harvest" today sends our thoughts in the same direction, although, as people from highly industrialized countries, we can hardly imagine anymore what the ripening and harvesting of the fruits of the earth once meant for the farmer and people in general.

The knowledge of the truth is of basic importance for the formation of one's personality and for the building of the inner human being. Man can only be truly mature with the truth and in the truth. In this lies the profound meaning and importance of education which the entire educational system from the schools to the universities must serve.

With the image of grain ripening for harvest, Christ wants to indicate the inner growth and maturation of man.

Man is bound by and dependent upon his own nature. At the same time he towers above it with the inner nature of his personal being. Thus, human maturation is something different from the ripening of the fruits of nature. This does not involve only physical and intellectual effort. An important part of the maturation process in man involves the spiritual, the religious dimension of his being. When Christ speaks of the "harvest," He means that man must mature towards God and then in God Himself; in His kingdom, he will receive the fruit of his effort and maturation.

I would like to point out this truth of the Gospel to you young people of today, both with great seriousness and at the same time with cheerful hope. You have arrived at a particularly important and critical time in your lives, in which much, or perhaps even everything, that will determine your further development and your future will be decided.

The knowledge of the truth is of basic importance for the formation of one's personality and for the building of the inner human being. Man can only be truly mature with the truth and in the truth. In this lies the profound meaning and importance of education which the entire educational system from the schools to the universities must serve. They must help young people to know and understand the world and themselves; they must help them to see what gives the existence and the works of man in the world their full meaning. For that reason education must also help them to know God. Man cannot live without knowing the significance of this existence.

STRENGTH TO BUILD
A MORE HUMAN WORLD

2. This search, finding of directions, and maturing with the basic and full truth of reality is, however, not easy. It has always been necessary to overcome numerous difficulties. It is apparently this problem that St. Paul refers to when he writes in his Second Epistle to the Thessalonians: "We beg you...not to be quickly shaken in mind or excited.... Let no one deceive you in any way...!" (2 Thes. 2:1-3) These words, addressed to a new group of the earliest Christians, must be reread today against the different background of our modern civilization and culture. Thus, I would like to call out to you young people of today: Do not be discouraged! Do not be deceived!

Be thankful if you have good parents who encourage and direct you onto the right path. Perhaps there are more of them than you can recognize at first sight. However, many young people suffer from their parents, feel that their parents do not understand them, or even abandon them. Others have to find the path to faith without, or even against, the will of their parents. Many suffer as a result of the "achievement pressures" in the schools, and encounter insecurity with respect to the prospects for a professional future. Should one not be afraid that technical and economic development will destroy man's natural living conditions? And anyway, what will be the future of our world which is divided into military power blocs, poor and rich nations, free and totalitarian states? Again and again wars flare up in this or that part of the world, causing death and misery to men. And then in many parts of the world, near and far, acts of the rawest kind of violence and bloody terror are carried out. Even here, where we commemorate before God the victims who were recently injured or suddenly killed on the edge of this large square by an explosive charge. It is hard to understand what man is capable of doing in the confusion of his mind and his heart.

It is against this background that we hear the call of the Gospel: "We beg you...not to be quickly shaken in mind or excited...!" All of these troubles and difficulties are part of the resistance with which we must nurture and test our growth in the fundamental truth. From this we derive the strength to help build a more just and more human world; from it we derive the readiness and courage to assume a growing measure of responsibility in the life of our society, state and Church. There is truly great consolation in the fact that, despite many shadows and darkness, there is a lot of good. The fact that too little is said of it does not mean that it is not there. Often one has to want to discover and recognize the good that is hidden. But it is at work and will perhaps at some later time become radiantly visible. Think, for example, what Mother Teresa of Calcutta had to do anonymously before a surprised world became aware of her work. Thus, I beg you not to be quickly shaken in mind or excited!

TEMPTATIONS TO FALL AWAY
FROM THE FAITH

3. However, is it not the case that in your society as you experience it in your surroundings, not a few who believe in Christ have become uncertain, or have lost their sense of orientation? And does that not have a particularly negative effect on young people? Does this not reveal something of the numerous temptations to fall away from the faith, of which the Apostle speaks in this Epistle?

The Word of God in today's liturgy gives us an idea of the broad scope of the loss of religious belief, such as seems to be emerging in our century, and makes its dimensions clear.

St. Paul writes: "For the mystery of lawlessness is already at work..." (2 Thes. 2:7). Would we not have to say that for our time as well? The mystery of lawlessness, falling away from God, has an inner structure and a definite dynamic gradation in the words of the Epistle of St. Paul: "...the man of lawlessness is revealed..., who opposes and exalts himself against every so-called god or object of worship so that he takes his seat in the temple of God proclaiming himself to be God" (2 Thes. 2:3-4). Thus, we have here an inner structure of negation, an uprooting of God in the heart of man and an uprooting of God in human society, with the aim, it is maintained, of obtaining a fuller "humanization" of man, i.e., making man human in a fuller sense of the word and in a certain way putting him in God's place, "deifying" him, as it were. This structure is very old and known to us from the first chapters of Genesis, i.e., the temptation of replacing the "divinity" (of the image and likeness of God), given to man by the Creator, with the "deification" of man against God, and without God, as is becoming visible under the atheistic conditions of many systems today.

Anyone who denies the fundamental truth of reality, who makes himself the measure of all things and, in doing so, puts himself in God's place; anyone who more or less consciously feels he can get along without God, the Creator of the world, without Christ, the Redeemer of man; anyone who, instead of seeking God, pursues idols, has always been fleeing from the sole, fundamental and saving truth.

There is also the attempt to escape by withdrawing into oneself. This can lead to giving up. "Nothing matters, anyway." If the disciples of Jesus had acted in this way, the world would never have heard anything of the redeeming Gospel of Christ. Withdrawing into oneself can assume the form of attempting to bring about an expansion of consciousness. Not a few young people here in your country are in the process of destroying their inner beings by withdrawing into themselves with the aid of alcohol and drugs. Very often anxiety and despair are the reasons behind this, but often, too, it is based on a thirst for pleasure, a lack of asceticism, or the irresponsible curiosity of wanting to "try out" everything once. Withdrawing into oneself can also lead to pseudo-religious sects, which abuse your idealism and your enthusiasm and deprive you of the freedom of thought and conscience. This also includes the attempt to escape through doctrines of salvation that pretend to be able to attain true happiness on the basis of certain external practices, but which, in the final analysis, throw the affected person back on himself and the unsolved problem of loneliness.

Then there is the attempt to flee from the fundamental truth by moving outwards, away from oneself, i.e., into political and social Utopias, idealized dreams of society. As necessary as ideals and aims are, utopian "magic formulae" will not get us anywhere, since they are usually accompanied by totalitarian power or the destructive use of violence.

THE GOOD SHEPHERD
LEADS IN TRUTH

4.   You can see all this happening, the numerous escape routes people take to fleé from the truth, the mysterious power of evil and iniquity that is at work. Are you never confronted with the temptations of isolation and despondency? There is an answer to this question in today's reading from the prophet Ezekiel. He speaks of a shepherd who follows his lost sheep into the wilderness in order to "rescue them from all places where they have been scattered on a day of clouds and thick darkness" (Ez. 34:12).

The shepherd who gathers up man on the dark path of his loneliness and disorientation and leads him back into the light is Christ. He is the Good Shepherd. He is ever present in the hidden place of the "mystery of iniquity," and Himself takes charge of the important matter of human existence on this earth. He does it in truth by freeing the heart of man from the fundamental contradiction contained in wanting to deify man without or against God, which creates a climate of isolation and disorientation. On the path leading out of the darkness of loneliness to true humanity, Christ, the Good Shepherd, in profound, pursuing and accompanying love, takes charge of every individual person, in particular every young person.

The prophet Ezekiel goes on to say of the Shepherd: "And I will bring them out from the peoples and gather them from the countries and will bring them into their own land; and I will feed them on the mountains of Israel, by the fountains and in all the inhabited places of the country" (Ez. 34:13). "I will seek the lost, and I will bring back the crippled, and I will strengthen the weak, and the fat and the strong I will watch over; I will feed them in justice" (Ez. 34:16).

In this way Christ wants to accompany the *maturing of man* in his humanity. He accompanies, nurtures and strengthens us in the life of His Church with His Word and in His sacraments, with the body and blood of His Passover Feast. He nurtures us as the immortal *Son of God,* lets man partake of His divine Sonship, "deifies" him within, so that he will become "human" in the full sense of the word, so that man, created in the image and likeness of God, will attain his maturity in God.

YOU ARE CALLED BY GOD

5. For this reason Christ says the harvest is "great." It is great. because of the immeasurable destiny of man. It is great because of the dignity of man. It is great in accordance with his calling. This wonderful harvest of the kingdom of God in human-

ity, the harvest of salvation in the history of man, peoples and nations is great. It is truly great, "but the laborers are few" (Mt. 9:37).

What does this mean? What is meant, dear young people, is that you have been called, called by God. My life, my human life is only meaningful if I have been called by God, in an important, decisive, final call. Only God can call man this way, no one but He. And this call of God constantly goes out, in and through Christ, to each and every one of you: To be workers in the harvest of your own humanity, workers in the vineyards of the Lord, in the Messianic harvest of humanity.

Jesus is in need of young people from your ranks who will follow His call and live as He did, poor and celibate, in order to be a living sign of the reality of God among your brothers and sisters.

God needs priests who will let themselves be led by the Good Shepherd into the service of His Word and His sacraments for men.

He needs people for the Catholic orders, men and women who will abandon everything in order to follow Him and in this way serve man.

He needs Christian married couples, who will render to each other and to their children service leading to full maturation of humanity in God.

God needs people who are ready to help and to serve the poor, the sick, the abandoned, the afflicted and spiritually wounded.

FOUR GREAT FIGURES

The glorious, more-than-1,000-year history of the Christian faith among your people is rich in individuals whose examples can provide an incentive in the fulfillment of your great calling. I would like to mention only four figures that come to me as a result of the present day and the city of Munich. There is St. Korbinian in the initial stages of the history of your faith in Christ, whose episcopal work laid the foundation for the Archdiocese of Munich-Freising. We are commemorating him in today's liturgy. There is the sainted Bishop Benno von Meissen, whose remains were laid to rest in Munich's *Frauenkirche*. He was a man of peace and reconciliation who preached nonviolence in his time, a friend of the poor and the distressed. In connection with the present day, Saint Elizabeth comes to mind, whose motto was: "Love, according to the Gospel." As the Princess of Wartburg she renounced all the privileges of her estate and devoted her life completely to the poor and the outcast. Finally, I would like to point out a man whom many of you or your parents knew personally: the Jesuit Father Rupert Mayer, at whose grave in the center of Munich, in the crypt of the *Bürgersaal*, many hundreds of people pause for a brief prayer every day. Despite the aftereffects of severe wounds he suffered on a patrol mission in the First World War, he openly and undauntedly stood up for the rights of the Church and for freedom at a difficult time in history, and as a result had to suffer the hardships of a concentration camp and exile.

Dear young people! Open your hearts to Christ's call! Your human life is a "unique adventure and enterprise," that can turn into both "a blessing and a curse." In view of you young people, who are the great hope of our future, let us ask the *"Lord of the harvest"* to send every one of you, and every one of

Dear young people! Open your hearts to Christ's call! In view of you young people, who are the great hope of our future, let us ask the "Lord of the harvest" to send every one of you, and every one of your young fellowmen on this earth, as laborers to His "great harvest," in keeping with the great wealth of callings and gifts in His kingdom on this earth.

your young fellowmen on this earth, as laborers to His "great harvest," in keeping with the great wealth of callings and gifts in His kingdom on this earth.

I would like to close with a special blessing for our Evangelical Lutheran brothers and sisters, who today in this country are celebrating their *Day of Repentance and Prayer*. This day is dominated for them by a knowledge of the necessity for constant renewal and by the calling of the Church to commemorate our communion as a people and as a State before God in prayer. The Roman Catholic Church is united with you in this matter. Please include your Catholic fellow-citizens, as well as your brother John Paul and his ministry, in your prayers this day. Amen.

GREATNESS
AND RESPONSIBILITY
OF ART
AND JOURNALISM

On Wednesday, November 19, the last day of the Pope's vist to Germany, he met with artists and journalists in Munich's "Herkules-Saal der Residenz." The Holy Father delivered the following address to these representatives of the world of culture.

Ladies and gentlemen,

I would like to extend a cordial greeting to the artists and journalists who have come to Munich from all parts of the Federal Republic of Germany on the occasion of my visit. I am pleased to be able to meet with you in this city which has always been a center of the arts and, in recent times, has also become an important center for the mass media. Our meeting today is intended to be a contribution to the dialogue between the Church and art, between the Church and the mass communications media. It is intended to contribute to a dialogue that had fallen silent for a long time or was marked by conflict and opposing views. In the following, I wish to point out a few unifying factors that exist between the Church and art, or the Church and journalism, and which might

be able to contribute to improving mutual understanding and to creating a fruitfully cooperative
relationship in the service of man.

EFFORTS OF MONASTERIES

1. The history of the relationship between the
Church, on the one hand, and art in architecture, the
visual arts, literature, the theater, and music, on the
other, has been eventful. If it had not been for the
efforts of the monasteries, for instance, the treasures
of ancient Greek and Latin authors would doubtless
not have been handed down to us. At that time the
Church showed great candor in its dialogue with
ancient literature and culture. For a long time the
Church was considered the mother of the arts. It was
the Church which commissioned art. The contents of
the Christian faith determined the motifs and themes
of art. How true this is can easily be demonstrated by
stopping to think what would remain if one removed
everything connected with religious and Christian
inspiration from European and German art history.

In recent centuries, most strongly since about
1800, the connection between the Church and culture, and thus between the Church and art, has grown
more tenuous. This took place in the name of autonomy and was intensified in the name of progressive
secularization. A chasm was opened up between the
Church and art that grew broader and deeper as time
went on. This difference was most obvious in the
areas of literature, the theater, and later, the film.
This mutual estrangement was increased by criticism
of the Church and Christianity, indeed, of religion in
general. The Church, for its part, which is fairly

understandable, became distrustful of the modern spirit and its many forms of expression. This spirit was considered inimical to the Faith and to the Church, critical of revelation and religion. The Church reacted by manifesting defensiveness, aloofness and opposition in the name of the Christian faith.

NEW RELATIONSHIP

2. An altogether new relationship between the Church and the world, between the Church and modern culture, and thus between the Church and art, was created by the Second Vatican Council. It can be described as a relationship characterized by attentiveness, openness and dialogue. Connected with this is the attentiveness to present-day matters, the *aggiornamento*. The Council Fathers dedicate an entire chapter (nos. 53-63) of the pastoral constitution *Gaudium et spes* to the proper promotion of cultural progress and, as in the old Church, approach the problem openly and without fear. The world is an independent reality, with its own autonomy. This includes the autonomy of culture and, with it, that of art. Correctly understood, this autonomy is not a protest against God or against the statements of the Christian faith. It is, rather, an expression of the fact that the world is God's own creation released in freedom, entrusted to man for his culture and in his responsibility.

Thus, the condition is given in which the Church can enter into a relationship of partnership, freedom and dialogue. The fact that art is free in your country and can be created and develop in freedom makes this relatively easy and, possibly, very fruitful. As concerns the responsible freedom of your professions, the Church will and must always be your partner, your partner in our common concern for the dignity of man in a world shaken in its foundations.

MAN, A CREATURE OF GOD

3. The Church defines the work of artists and journalists in a manner that emphasizes the central importance, the greatness and the responsibility of your professions. According to Christian belief every man was created in the image and likeness of God. In view of the creative nature of their work, this is especially true of artists and journalists. Yours are creative professions, each in accordance with its specific function. You give form to reality and the material of the world. You do not make do with merely reproducing images or giving surface descriptions. You attempt to "thicken" the reality of man and his world in the original sense of the word. Using words, sound, pictures and structured form you want to get across, make perceptible, some of the truth and profundity of the world and of man, including the negative sides of human life.

Saying this does not imply a secret Christian or Church desire to move into the field of art and artists, the media and journalists, but rather an appraisal of the situation from the standpoint of the Christian faith, an appraisal that is filled with positiveness, respect and recognition. The German Cardinal Nikolaus von Kues once wrote: "Creativity and art, when they happen to occur in a soul, are not that essential art which is God, but they are communication of and participation in it."

APPRAISAL OF SITUATION

4. The question arises: where are the mutual connections between the Church and art, the Church and journalism? The answer to this is: the subject of the Church and the subject of both artists and journalists is man, the image of man, the truth of man, the *"ecce homo,"* including his history, his world and environment, as well as the social, economic and political context.

As the conveyor of the message of Christian faith, the Church will always speak out in reminder of the fact that the reality of man cannot be fully described without the theological dimension; that it must not be forgotten that man is a creature of God, limited in time and space, dependent upon assistance; that human life was given and received; and that man is in search of meaning and salvation, because he is in many ways caught up in constraints and guilt. The Church will always remind people of the fact that the true image of man and the human is given in Jesus Christ. Jesus Christ, according to the German philosopher Karl Jaspers, will remain the most significant figure in history. And the Council emphasized: "Christ the new Adam,...makes man fully known to man himself and reveals to him his highest calling" *(Gaudium et spes,* no. 22).

Art, too, in all of its sectors, including television and film, is concerned with man, the image of man and the truth of man. Although appearances often seem to contradict this, these profound characteristics and interests are not altogether foreign to modern art, either. The religious and Christian wellspring of art has never quite run dry. Themes such as guilt and mercy, bondage and redemption, injustice and justice, charity and freedom, solidarity and love for one's fellowman, hope and consolation, are recurrent in modern literature and film scripts, and have received great acclaim. A partnership between the Church and art with an eye to man consists in the fact that both wish to free man from bondage and lead him back to himself. They open up an area of freedom for him, freedom from the constraints of utility, achievement at any cost, effectiveness, prior planning and functionalism.

SERVICE TO THE CHURCH

5. We said that the Church and art were concerned with man, his image, his truth, the revelation of his reality, and this in the present process of *"aggiornamento,"* to use a word of the Second Vatican Council.

In this task art renders the Church a great service, that of concretizing. The Church is dependent on this service, since the truth is concrete. In modern art, in literature and the theater, in the visual arts, in film and in large areas of journalism, man is derobed of all romantic trappings and radiance. He is, one could say, described in unadorned reality. In modern art this includes pointing out aberrations and confusion, anxiety and despair, absurdity and meaninglessness, the depiction of history and the world as something that has degraded to the level of caricature. This is often connected with the removal of all taboos.

Today, literature, the theater, film, and the visual arts see their function largely in terms of criticism, protest, opposition, and pointing an accusing finger at existing conditions. The beautiful as a category of art seems to have fallen by the wayside in favor of depictions of man in his negative aspects, in his contradictions, in his hopelessness, and in the absence of meaning. This seems to be the current *"ecce homo."* The so-called "intact world" is an object of scorn and cynicism. These questions, too, were dealt with with great candor by the Second Vatican Council in its decree on social means of communication *(Inter mirifica).*

The Christian faith and the Christian Church do not object to the depiction of evil in its various forms. Evil is a reality whose extent has been experienced and suffered in this century in the extreme by your country and mine. Without the reality of evil, the reality of good, redemption, mercy and salvation cannot be measured. This is not a license for evil, but rather an indication of its position.

In this context an important and potentially dangerous matter should be pointed out. Can the reflection of the negative in the broad variety of modern art not turn into an end in itself? Can it not lead to enjoyment of evil, pleasure in destruction, cynicism and misanthropy?

When the reality of evil is depicted, the intention of art is to show the horrible as being horrible and to move the viewer or reader. As such, an artistic depiction of evil does not aim at leaving the situation unchanged, but rather improving it. You must change your life, you must turn back and begin again, you must resist evil so that it will not have the last word and become determining reality. This is not only an appeal and warning of the Church; it is also the task of art and journalism in all areas, and not merely on the basis of a moral burden. Helping, healing, purging and purifying power was ascribed to art by the Greeks. There should be encouragement for hope in the attempt to find meaning in life, even though not all questions as to the whys and wherefores of human existence can be answered. All this must not be lost in modern art, for its own sake and for the sake of man. In this service to man there can be and should be a connection between the Church and art, without need for either side to lose any of its own identity.

CHURCH NEEDS ART, NEEDS IMAGES

6. If the Church is intent on *"aggiornamento,"* i.e., modernization of the Christian faith, its directives and promises, then it must be said that nowhere is the situation, the atmosphere of the times, and the range of questions occupying the mind of contemporary man, so impressively depicted as in modern art and journalism. The Church has to turn to and is dependent on this source of information. If the Christian faith is to be conveyed as a hopeful message and as an answer for man, then the pertinent questions must be formulated and an awareness of them created.

The Church needs art. It needs art to convey its own message. The Church also needs the *word* that gives testimony of the Word of God and at the same time is the word of man, that will fit into the linguistic world of contemporary man, as found in modern art and journalism. Only in this way will the Word remain alive and move man.

The Church needs *images.* The Gospel is told by making use of many images and parables. Images can and should be used for illustrative purposes. In the New Testament Christ is called the image, the icon of the invisible God. The Church is not only the Church of the word, but also of the sacraments, the holy signs and symbols. Images have always been used with the word to convey the message of salvation. And that is the way it should be. Faith is not affected only by hearing, but also by seeing, by both basic senses of man.

Music, such as used in holy Mass, is also placed in the service of the Faith. Everyone knows that many great works of music owe their existence to the living faith of the Church and its liturgical practices. Faith not only needs to be confessed and spoken; it also needs to be sung. And music indicates that the matter of faith is also a matter of joy, love, reverence and exuberance. This motivation and inspiration is still alive today. In many cases new forms of music are being sought as a result of the liturgical reform. Here an ample field is open for development. The connection between the Church and art is alive and fruitful in the area of music.

Something similar can be said of the relationship of the Church to *architecture* and to the *visual arts.* The Church requires indoor space to house the gatherings of the People of God in its many activities. After the horrible destruction of the last World War, a new style of church architecture was developed, especially in the Federal Republic of Germany, that provides testimony of a living Church. Modern church architecture has consciously wanted to avoid imitating the Romanesque, Gothic, Renaissance, Baroque and Rococo styles, most German examples of which are located in Bavaria. Modern church architecture wanted to give form and expression to the faith of our time with the means available to us today and on the basis of the contemporary spirit and sense of style, and at the same time to give it a religious atmosphere. There are many successful examples of this. I would like to thank everyone involved in this great endeavor, the architects and artists, the theologians and construction workers, the pastors and the laity.

INVITATION TO ALL CREATIVE ARTISTS

7. The Church needs art. It needs it in many ways. *But does art also need the Church?* It seems largely not to be the case these days. But if the relationship between religion, the Church, and art is so close as I have tried to show, especially with respect to man, the image of man and his truth, and if the content of Christian faith taught by the Church inspired art in its greatest periods and in works unsurpassed to this day, including those in Germany, allow me to ask the question: will art not be poorer, is it not losing important themes and motifs by doing without the reality represented by the Church?

My meeting with you today is intended to be a sincere invitation to all creative artists to enter into a new cooperative partnership based on mutual confidence, an invitation to rediscover the profound intellectual and religious dimensions that have distinguished art in its highest and most noble forms of expressions at all times.

GRATEFUL FOR SERVICE TO THE FAITH

8. My reflections thus far have included the broad spectrum of media journalists working for press, radio and television.

Planning and organizing the Papal visit to the Federal Republic of Germany was assisted by the media, i.e., by you, the journalists. You are covering it on the spot in résumés and in commentaries which indicate, for the most part, your favor and approval. For all of this I wish to express my sincere thanks. Through your work, what is taking place in but a few cities of the Federal Republic of Germany is reproduced millions of times. Never before in history has the spreading of the Gospel had such an opportunity to reach so many people. For this service, a service to the Faith, to the Church, and thus a service to man, I wish to repeat my thanks.

This occasion makes it clear to everyone the power placed in your hands, in the hands of journalists. They have a huge influence on the public, on the formation of public opinion, and on the consciousness of millions. The words and the pictures that you convey of the reality of the world, of man, of society, or also of the Christian faith and of the Church, determines the judgment, behavior and actions of many people.

In reaction to the central control and abuse of the press under National Socialism, it was possible to establish a pluralistic press system in the Federal Republic of Germany. In view of the fact that there are numerous political and philosophical differences, the journalist is constantly confronted with the task of dealing with convictions and positions, recognizing and exposing ideological tendencies and the necessity to clarify and define his own standpoint. This great opportunity provided by freedom involves an equally large responsibility. The information and news commentary of the press should always be characterized by objectivity, critical judgment, and a sense of justice. The danger of slanting the news oneself is just as evident as the danger of giving priority to sensational news. There are many regrettable examples of this in the tabloid press. The effects of the journalist are put to the test precisely in the area of news policy. The importance of his responsibility can hardly be overestimated. The journalist cannot sufficiently exercise this responsibility unless he has clear moral convictions and a sense of the great importance of public communication in a free society.

MEDIA'S RESPONSIBILITY

9. The *responsibility of journalists* becomes especially clear when the effects of the media are taken into account. Part of the journalist's responsibility involves a constant awareness of the possible consequences of his work. Research on the effects of the media is still in the incipient stages. There are initial indications of the influence which violence in the media has on young people. It seems to be correct that the media are not alone responsible for the kind and degree of influence, but they cannot self-complacently deny the role they do play. Journalists, along with families and educators, are called upon to take cognizance of the damaging effects of showing violence in the media and to help to prevent this.

The situation is similar in the case of promoting political knowledge in the public. Here, too, the media are embedded in a network of relations. The responsible journalist must be aware of the possibilities he has of contributing to the cultivation of political awareness, more objective coverage and more consideration of the personal values of others.

An analysis of moral value trends clearly indicates that the media play a leading role, especially television. On a broad front the media have helped to bring about a change in attitudes, norms, and moral constraints in the area of sexual behavior, both among young people and adults, in current views on marriage and family and their current state, and in the raising of children. Many of the attitudinal changes that the media have helped to bring about have given people more freedom in social intercourse, perhaps making interpersonal relations more profound. However, what is today all too clearly evident and is perhaps not given enough attention by those working in the media, is the fact that alleged greater freedom results in moral laxity; moral obligations are given up in favor of new constraints that no longer do justice to man in all of his dignity; and confidence in personal relations is weakened. The media are certainly not solely responsible for this, but they have helped to initiate and strengthen the process.

The journalist is called upon to acquire a better knowledge of the effects of his work and not to close his eyes to them. Only when it is combined with conscientiousness and responsibility, the power placed in his hands is not dangerous. The yardstick for good journalistic work should not be its effect on the public, but rather truth and justice. In this you serve the cause of your profession and at the same time you serve and help man.

For this authentic service to truth and man in art and journalism, I wish and request with all my heart for you who are present and all of your fellow journalists God's illumination and assistance.

IN YOUR OLD AGE, ACCOMPANY CHRIST TO THE CROSS

On Wednesday, November 19, in the cathedral in Munich, the Holy Father met with representatives of a notable part of the German populace—the elderly. The Pope offered them the following message.

My dear brothers and sisters who are advanced in age!

It fills me with special joy that during my visit to Germany I am allowed to meet with you in a special hour of prayer. I come as to familiar friends; for I know that in my service I am supported in a special way by your concern, prayer, and sacrifice. So I greet you here in the Cathedral of Our Lady in Munich with heartfelt gratitude. Especially I thank you for the profound words of welcome and for your prayer by which you accompanied me during these days. Together with you I greet all the people of your age group in your country, especially those who through radio and television are united with us in this moment. *Grüss Gott* to all of you who longer than I have "endured the work and heat of the day" (Mt. 20:12), who longer than I have exerted yourselves to meet the Lord and to serve Him in all fidelity, in the great things and in the small ones, in joy and in suffering!

1. The Pope bows with devotion before old age, and he invites all people to do the same with him. Old age is the crown of the steps of life. It gathers in the harvest, the harvest from what you have learned and experienced, the harvest from what you have done and achieved, the harvest from what you have suffered and undergone. As in the finale of a great symphony, all the great themes of life combine to a mighty harmony. And this harmony bestows wisdom —the wisdom which young King Solomon is praying for (cf. 1 Kgs. 3:9-11) and which means more to him than power and riches, more than beauty and health (cf. Wis. 7:7, 8, 10)—the wisdom about which we read in the rules of life of the Old Testament: "How attractive is wisdom in the aged, and understanding and counsel in honorable men! Rich experience is the crown of the aged, and their boast is the fear of the Lord" (Sir. 25:5f.).

To today's older generation, that is to you, my dear brothers and sisters, this crown of wisdom is due in a very special way: some of you had in *two* world wars to see and to endure immense pain; many of you have thereby lost your relatives, your health, your profession, your house and your home country; you have come to know the abyss of the human heart, but also its ability for heroic willingness to help, and for loyalty to the Faith, as well as its power to dare a new beginning.

Wisdom confers distance, but not a distance which stands aloof from the world; it allows people to be above things, *without despising them;* it allows us to see the world with the eyes—and with the heart!—of God. It allows us with God to say "yes" even to our limitations, even to our past—with its disappointments, omissions, and sins. For "we know that in everything God works for good with those who love him" (Rom. 8:28). From the conciliative power of this wisdom spring up kindness, patience, understanding, and—that precious ornament of age—the sense of humor.

You yourselves know best, my dear sisters and brothers, that this precious harvest of life which the Creator has apportioned to you is not an uncontested possession. It requires vigilance, carefulness, self-control, and sometimes even a resolute battle. Otherwise it is endangered, easily to be eaten away or to be corroded by idleness, by moods, by superficiality, by arrogance, or even by bitterness. Do not lose heart; with the grace of our Lord start over and over again, and use the sources of power which He offers you: in the sacraments of the Bread and of Forgiveness; in the Word which comes to you in sermons and in reading and in spiritual conversation! In this place I am sure that I am allowed also in your name most cordially to thank the priests who reserve a decisive place in their work and in their hearts for the pastoral work among the aged. In this way they at the same time render the best service to their whole community; for thereby they win for it, in a sense, a legion of faithful intercessors.

Next to the priests who serve you with their pastoral work I should like to address myself to the priests of your age group. My dear confrères! The Church thanks you for your lifelong work in the vineyard of the Lord. To the younger priests Jesus says in the Gospel of John (4:38): "Others have labored, and you have entered into their labor." Most venerable priests, keep on bringing the needs of the Church

before God through your priestly service of prayer
— *"Then I will go to the altar of God, to God my exceeding joy"!* (Ps. 43:4)

A TREASURE TO THE CHURCH

2. Brothers and sisters of the older generation, you are a treasure for the Church, you are a blessing for the world! How often you have to relieve the young parents, how well you know how to introduce the youngsters to the history of your family and of your home country, to the tales of your people and to the world of faith! The young adults with their problems often find an easier way to you than to their parents' generation. To your sons and daughters you are the most precious support in their hours of difficulty. With your advice and your engagement you cooperate in many committees, associations and initiatives of ecclesiastical and public life.

You are a necessary complement in a world which shows enthusiasm for the vitality of youth and for the power of the so-called "best years," in a world where what can be counted counts so much. You remind it that it continues building upon the diligence of those who have been young and strong *earlier,* and that one day it, too, will place its work in younger hands. In you it becomes apparent that the meaning of life cannot consist in earning and spending money, that in all our external activities there has to mature something internal, and something eternal in all the temporal—according to the words of Saint Paul: "Though our outer nature is wasting away, our inner nature is being renewed every day" (2 Cor. 4:16).

Indeed, old age deserves our devotion, a devotion which also shines forth from Holy Scripture when it places before our eyes Abraham and Sarah, when it calls Simeon and Anna to the Holy Family in the temple, when it calls the priests "elders" (Acts 14:23; 15:2; 1 Tm. 4:14; 5:17, 19; Ti. 1:5; 1 Pt. 5:1), when it sums up the worship of the whole of creation in the adoration of the twenty-four elders, and when finally God calls Himself: "the Ancient of Days" (Dn. 7:9, 22).

ACCEPT THE BURDEN OF OLD AGE

3. Is it possible to intone a higher song in honor of the dignity of old age? But, my dear elder listeners, I am sure you would be disappointed if the Pope would not also mention another aspect of becoming old; if he would have brought you only—maybe unexpected—the honors, but would have failed to bring you consolation. Just as to the beautiful season in which we are not only belongs the harvest and the solemn splendor of color, but also the branches being stripped of their leaves, the leaves falling and decaying; not only the soft and full light, but also the wet and dreary fog, in the same way old age is not only the strong final accord or the conciliative sum of life, but also the time of fading, a time where the world becomes strange and life can turn into a burden, and the body into pain. And so I add to my call, "Be aware of your dignity," the other one, "Accept your burden."

For most people the burden of old age means in the first place a certain frailty of the body; the senses are no longer as acute, the limbs no longer as pliable as they used to be, the organs become more sensitive (cf. Sir. 12:3f.). The things one may experience in younger years in days of sickness, often become one's daily—and nightly!—companions in old age. One is forced to give up many activities which used to be familiar and dear.

Also, the memory may refuse its service: new facts are no longer received easily, and old ones fade away. And so the world ceases to be familiar; the world of one's own family with the living and working conditions of the adults utterly changed, with the interests and forms of expression of young people so completely different, with the new learning goals and methods of the children. The home-country becomes strange with its growing cities, the increasing density of population, and the landscape many times remodeled. The world of politics and economics turns strange, the world of social and medical care becomes anonymous and unintelligible. And even that domain where we should feel at home most of all—the Church in her life and doctrine—has become strange to many of you through her effort to meet the demands of the time and the expectations and needs of the younger generation.

By this world which is hard to understand, you feel misunderstood and often enough rejected. Your opinion, your cooperation, your presence is not asked for—that is how you feel and how, unfortunately, sometimes it actually is.

A REDEEMING SUFFERING

4. What can the Pope say to this? How shall I console you? I do not want to take it too easy. I do not

want to belittle the anxieties of old age, your weaknesses and illnesses, your helplessness and loneliness. But I would like to see them in a conciliatory light—in the light of our Savior "who for us did sweat blood, who for us was scourged at the pillar, who for us was crowned with thorns." In the trials of old age He is the Companion of your pain and you are His companions on His way of the cross. There is no tear you have to shed alone, and none you shed in vain (cf. Ps. 5:9). By this suffering He has redeemed suffering, and through your suffering you cooperate in His salvation (cf. Col. 1:24). Accept your suffering as His embrace and turn it into a blessing by accepting it from the hand of the Father who in His inscrutable, yet unquestionable wisdom and love is using just this to bring about your perfection. It is in the furnace that metal turns into gold (cf. 1 Pt. 1:7); it is in the press that the grape becomes wine.

In this spirit—which God alone can give us—it becomes also easier to be understanding with those who through negligence, carelessness, heedlessness, contribute to cause our need, and it becomes possible for us to forgive also those who knowingly and even intentionally make us suffer without, however, completely conceiving how much pain they cause us. "Father, forgive them, for they do not know what they are doing!" (Lk. 23:34) Also with regard to us has this word been spoken which alone brings salvation.

MODEL IN ST. ELIZABETH

5. In this Spirit—whom we want to implore together and for each other in this hour—we are also

going to be awake and grateful for all loving thoughts, words, and deeds which we receive each day, which we so easily get used to and which, therefore, we easily take for granted and which we overlook. We are celebrating the feast of St. Elizabeth, a saint your nation has given to the whole world as a symbol of self-sacrificing charity. She is the sublime example and great patroness for all who serve their fellow creatures in need—be it through their profession or on a volunteer basis; be it in the circle of their friends and relatives—and who meet Christ in them, whether they know it or not. That, my dear elder people, is the reward which you give to those for whom you dislike being a burden. You are the occasion for them to meet the Lord, the opportunity to outgrow themselves, and by your turning to them you let them share in the already mentioned fruits of life which God allowed to mature in you! Therefore, do not bury your requests in a timid, disappointed or reproachful heart, but express them in all naturalness—being convinced of your own dignity and of the good in the hearts of the others. And be happy over each opportunity to practice that royal word of "Thank you" which rises from all altars and which is going to fill our eternal beatitude.

And so I am sure that I will be allowed together with you to thank all those people who work for the well-being of the older generation, for their well-being in body and mind, in order to help them find a fulfilled life and a permanent home in society, all those who work in the many ecclesiastical, civil and public organizations, associations, and initiatives, on a communal or on a higher level, in legislature and administration, or just on a private basis. I commend especially the fact that working *for* the elder people is becoming more and more working *with* the elder people.

SOMEONE STILL POORER

6. With this I turn again to you, my elder brothers and sisters, and to the consolation you expect from me. There is a saying: "When you are lonely, go and visit somebody who is still lonelier than you!" This wisdom I would like to recommend to you. Open your mind for those companions on your road who in whatever respect are in a still poorer condition than you, whom you can help in one way or the other— through a conversation, through giving a hand, some favor, or at least your expressed sympathy! I promise to you in the name of Jesus: in this you are going to find strength and consolation (cf. Acts 20:35).

In this way you simultaneously practice in small matters what we all are as a whole. We are one body in many members: those who bring help and those who receive help; those who are more healthy and those who are more sick; those who are younger and those who are older; those who have stood the test of life, those who are still standing it, and those who just are growing into it; those who are young and those who once have been young; those who are old and those who are going to be old tomorrow. We all together represent the fullness of the Body of Christ, and we all together mature into this fullness—"into the perfect Man, fully mature with the fullness of Christ" (Eph. 4:13).

CONSCIOUS OF DEATH

7. The last consolation we are seeking together, my dear fellow pilgrims "in this vale of tears" *(Salve Regina)*, is the consolation in the face of death. Since our birth we have been going to meet it, but in our old age we become more conscious of its approaching from year to year—if only we do not forcefully suppress it from our thoughts and feelings. The Creator has arranged it so that in old age accepting and standing the test of death is being prepared, made easier and learned in an almost natural manner. Because becoming old, as we have seen, means a slow taking leave of the unbroken fullness of life, of the unimpeded contact with the world.

The great school of living and dying then brings us to many an open grave; it makes us stand at many a deathbed before it will be us around whom other people will be standing in prayer—so may God grant it. An old person has experienced such lessons of life in a greater number than young ones do, and he is seeing them with increasing frequency. That is his great advantage on the way to that great threshold which we often in a biased way conceive of as being an abyss and night.

The view across the threshold is dark from our side; but to those who have gone before us God will allow in His love to accompany our lives and to surround us with care more often than we possibly think. It has been the conviction of deep and living faith which gave to a church in this city the name of "All Souls' Church." And the two German churches in Rome are called: Santa Maria in Campo Santo and Santa Maria dell'Anima. The more the fellow beings of our visible world reach the limits of their ability to help, the more we should see the messengers of the love of God in those who already have passed the test of death and who are now waiting for us over there: the saints, especially our personal patrons, and our deceased relatives and friends whom we hope are at home in God's mercy.

Many of you, my dear sisters and brothers, have lost the visible presence of your partner. To you I direct my pastoral admonition. Allow God ever more to be the partner of your lives; then you will also be united to the one whom He gave you as a companion once upon a time and who himself now has found in God his center.

Without familiarity with God there is in the last end no consolation in death. For that is exactly what God intends with death, that at least in this one sublime hour of our life we allow ourselves to fall into His love without any other security than just this love of His. How could we show Him our faith, our hope, our love in a more lucid manner!

One last consideration in this context. I am sure it echoes the conviction of many a heart. Death itself is a consolation! Life on this earth, even if it were no "vale of tears" could not offer a home to us forever. It would turn more and more into a prison, an "exile" (*Salve Regina*). "For all that passes is just a parable!" (Goethe, *Faust II*, final chorus) And so the words of St. Augustine which never lose their color come to our lips: "You have created us for Yourself, Lord; and our heart is restless until it finds its rest in You!" (*Confessiones I*, 1, 1)

And so there are not those who are destined to die and those who stand in the so-called life. What is awaiting all of us is a birth, a transformation whose pains we fear with Jesus on the Mount of Olives, but whose radiant exit we already carry within ourselves, since at our Baptism we have been submerged into the death and victory of Jesus (cf. Rom. 6:3-6; Col. 2:12).

Together with all of you, together with you here in our Lady's cathedral, with you before radio and television, with all those whom I was allowed to meet in these blessed days, with all the citizens and guests of this beautiful country, with all those who believe, and for all those who are seeking, with the children and young people, with the adults and the old people, I would like in this hour of farewell to turn our meditation into prayer!

"Upon you I have leaned from my birth; forsake me not when my strength is spent!" (Ps. 71:6, 9)

"Come to our aid with your mercy and keep us safe from temptation and sin, so that we may be full of confidence as we await the coming of our Savior Jesus Christ!" (Order of the Mass)

And here in our Lady's cathedral I would like to combine our prayer which always is spoken in the Spirit of Jesus and only through Jesus arrives at the Father, with the prayer of the one who, being the first to have been saved, is our mother and our sister (Paul VI at the conclusion of the third session of the Council, *Insegnamenti* II, pp. 675 and 664):

"Holy Mary, Mother of God, pray for us sinners now and at the hour of our death! Amen."

Amen. Praised be Jesus Christ!

PEACE AND UNITY
OF CHRISTIANS

On Wednesday, November 19, the Pope ended his pastoral visit to the Federal Republic of Germany. At the airport in Munich, the Holy Father delivered the final message of this pilgrimage.

Most honorable Mr. President of the Republic;
Your Eminence the Cardinal;
Dear brothers in the episcopal ministry;
Ladies and gentlemen:

1. My pastoral visit through the German country is approaching its end. At the moment of my departure I would like to express my sincere gratitude: *gratitude towards God and men* for the gift of this singular event.

I beg you very cordially, most honorable Mr. President, to accept my profound gratitude for the extremely friendly reception given to me at the individual stations of my visit and by the citizens of your country.

I would like to thank in a very special way the innumerable helpers who for weeks have labored intensively and so successfully for the external organization of this trip and who in its course surely must have worked overtime. I am thinking here above all of the city governments, the police, the border security force *(Bundesgrenzschutz)*—especially the pilots of the helicopters—the auxiliaries of Malta *(Malteser Hilfsdienst)*, the travel agencies, as well as the local committees of the individual dioceses. To all of them a very cordial *"Gott-Vergelt's"* (May God reward you)!

During this trip we have been reminded of important stations in the history of the Church and the people of this country. I have been conscious of the fact that I was making a pilgrimage through a land whose Christian roots reach back to the time of the Romans; a land in which in the eighth century the holy bishop and martyr Boniface laid the foundation of this local Church; a land from which during the Middle Ages came a series of Popes and emperors, of saints and scholars who have been of historical importance. It is the land where 700 years ago St. Albert with the surname of "the Great" passed away, and where 450 years ago the *"Confessio Augustana"* was promulgated.

2. While I recall with devotion the more remote past with some of its most prominent landmarks, I cannot pass over the events of more recent history. Not too long ago, in September of 1978 to be precise, I was then here in your country in my capacity as Archbishop and Cardinal of Krakow, together with a delegation of Polish bishops. That visit took place just a few weeks after the election of Pope John Paul I and—who would have thought of it?—just a few days before his death. Just so, nobody could anticipate that divine Providence would soon thereafter charge me to take over after him the heritage of the See of Peter.

There are two motives which cause me to mention these remote and recent historical events here at my departure. The first motive consists in the fact that the visit of the Polish bishops under the direction of the Primate of Poland gave evidence to a very important development which was going on between your country and mine, and which is still going on: I mean that process whose goal it is to overcome the tragic results of World War II, especially those results which have put their imprint upon the hearts of men. I know them from my own experience because I have lived with my own nation through the cruel reality of this World War. In this context I am very grateful for the return visit which recently a group of Cardinals and bishops of your country have paid to Poland, a visit which I have been allowed to return through my pastoral visit to you.

Indeed, that is what it is all about! We must do everything possible in order to give a new foundation and new form to the life and union of the people and the nations of this continent, and thereby to overcome the results of that terrible experience of our century. The martyrs and saints of all ages up to Blessed Maximilian Kolbe have shown us that "the love of Christ is more powerful," as it was expressed by the motto of the last *"Katholikentag"* in Berlin. According to this principle the building of a better future for the nations and for man is not only possible, but constitutes for us a grave obligation: it is the most urgent task of our age in this second millennium after Christ which has already entered into its last phase.

Therefore I am so grateful for the invitation to this pastoral visit which I was able to undertake in this year in order to give to you my service as Bishop of Rome and Succcessor of St. Peter.

3. The second motive for my foregoing considerations consists in this, that from the invitation extended to me first by the Cardinal of Cologne and then by all the Cardinals and bishops together, I not only perceived a special call of the remote and recent past, but also the challenge for the future whose direction has been indicated by the teaching and the spirit of the Second Vatican Council. Especially in your country where Martin Luther was born and where the *"Confessio Augustana"* was promulgated 450 years ago, it seems to me that this challenge for the future is extremely important and decisive.

What kind of future are we talking about? It is that future which for us as disciples of Christ comes from the prayer of Jesus in the room of the Last Supper, the prayer: I ask you, Father "that all may be one" (Jn. 17:21). This prayer of the Lord becomes for us all the source of a new life and a new longing. As Bishop of Rome and Successor of St. Peter I put myself fully and completely in the stream of this longing; in it I recognize the language of the Holy Spirit and the will of Christ whom I wish to obey and to be faithful to in everything.

I want to serve unity; I want to walk all the ways in which, after the experiences of the centuries and millennia, Christ is leading us towards the unity of that flock where He alone is the only and reliable Good Shepherd.

That is why it was my great wish to make this visit just in this ecumenically so important jubilee year. Therefore I would like to thank cordially the Council of the Evangelical Church in Germany and the Study Group of Christian Churches for taking part in the meeting with the Pope and for taking up the dialogue with me in their own country.

I hold the firm hope that the unity of Christians is already on its way in the power of the Spirit of truth and love. We know how long the times of separation and division have been. We do not know how long the way to unity will be. But one thing we know with all the greater certainty: We have to keep on walking this way with perseverance—keep on going and do not stand still! There are many things we have to do for it; above all, we have to persevere in prayer, in an ever more powerful and intimate prayer. Unity can be given only as a gift of the Lord, as the fruit of His passion and resurrection, in the "fullness of time" appointed to it.

"Watch and pray" (Mt. 26:41) in the garden of Gethsemane of the numerous experiences of history so that you do not fall into temptation, and stay on the right way!

4. Again I would like to thank you, very honorable Mr. President of the Republic, and all representatives of the public authority for the invitation extended to me.

As my farewell I offer my blessings to all the citizens of your country, including all your German brothers and sisters who are living across the borders of your country, and all those who in some instances have emigrated generations ago to different countries of the earth.

Allow me to combine these wishes with an invitation and a call. Since the last catastrophe of war, with its frightful pictures that have swept over Europe and our home countries, some time has already elapsed.

And yet, even today there has to be repeated over and over again the call for a future world which in the words of the Second Vatican Council should be "more conformed to the dignity of man," and that for all men on earth. You will agree with me that such a desire represents a challenge, because the world of man and life in it can be more conformed to human dignity only when man himself constantly exerts himself to be ever more worthy of his being man, and that in all areas and dimensions of his existence!

I shall owe deepest gratitude to divine Providence if this ardent desire is ever more fulfilled in your hearts and in your world, if it becomes ever more a reality for you and everybody among other people and nations. Likewise, I shall be grateful if you, sons and daughters of so important a nation, heirs of a prominent civilization and descendants of such great personalities in the history of Europe and the world, become ever more pioneers of that civilization of love which alone is able to let our world become ever more conformed to the dignity of man.

This is my last wish and blessing to you. It includes at the same time my gratitude for these days I was allowed to spend with you in your country.

May God bless this country and all its inhabitants!

ON RETURNING
TO ROME

On his return to Rome from the pastoral visit to the Federal Republic of Germany, on Wednesday, November 19, the Pope was met at Fiumicino Airport by a number of religious and civil authorities. After being welcomed home, the Holy Father delivered the following address.

Mr. Prime Minister,
Revered Cardinals,
Honored Ambassadors,
Beloved brothers and sisters,

1. Returning to Italian soil following the deep emotions of a brief but intensive journey, full of meetings and talks, I would like above all to express my gratitude to the Lord who permitted me to visit and speak personally with our dear brothers and sisters in Germany and with the government leaders of the country.

I was able, in fulfillment of the universal mission entrusted to me by Christ, to come into contact with the religious spirit and generous heart of that people, already well known to me. I was filled with admiration for their ancient tradition in the faith, the testimony I saw of human solidarity, the desire for

increasingly genuine Christian testimony. In addition, I observe the presence of profound ethical values, fundamental for true progress in the life of a society.

Thus, I am greatly satisfied with having accepted the invitation of the bishops and heads of government of the Federal Republic of Germany to pay a visit of such significance, carried out on the occasion of the 700th anniversary of the death of St. Albert the Great, Doctor of the Church and extraordinary representative of medieval culture, who is buried in St. Andrew's Church in Cologne.

2. A particularly outstanding moment of my visit was my meeting with scientists, scholars and students from the University of Cologne in Cologne Cathedral, the theme of which was dedicated to the *"Doctor universalis,"* considered by his contemporaries to be a *"vir in omni scientia divinus,"* exceptional as a scholar, a teacher, a priest, and a man of peace; a strong advocate of distinguishing between the humanities, the access to which does not require more than exposure to the light of reason; and theology, the study of the divine. My meeting in Mainz with the leaders of the other Christian denominations was very important from an ecumenical standpoint. Our meeting was held in the context of the commemoration of the 450th anniversary of the famous Augsburg Confession, which is still a reminder today for Christians of good will that they should go in search of the truth and the path leading to unity with a clear mind.

I am pleased to have had the opportunity to meet with immigrants from various countries, outstanding among them a large group of Italians, all of whom are contributing to the economic progress of the Federal Republic in the context of a new and growing European mentality. I was greatly pleased by my visit to Fulda, which involved meetings with bishops, priests and seminarians at the tomb of St. Boniface, apostle and founder of the Church in Germany, and reformer of the Franconian Church, which he closely connected with the Apostolic See. His burial site is still considered the religious center of Catholic Germany, where the German Bishops' Conference meets every year in memory of the values of the early days of the German Church, the lasting nature of ideals and the work of this great bishop and martyr.

I can still see before me the exultant crowd, thousands of faithful Christians in silent prayer, who wanted to pay a tribute of devotion to the Successor of St. Peter, thereby reaffirming their sentiments of profound communion with the Apostolic See that Christ wanted to be a firm foundation of truth and unity.

3. At the end of my journey I would like once again to extend my greetings and good wishes to the German people and take this opportunity to repeat my sincere thanks to the bishops and government leaders of the Federal Republic of Germany for their kind invitation and for the consideration they showed in supporting my pastoral endeavor and following my pilgrimage.

And now, Mr. Prime Minister, I would like to express my sincere gratitude and appreciation for the cordial words with which you have greeted my return in the name of the President of the Republic and of the Italian government. I would also like to address my respectful thanks to each of those present here: to the Cardinals, to the honorable representatives of the Italian State and government, to the distinguished members of the diplomatic corps, and to all those who have received me with their joyous welcome, to the heads of the airlines, the pilots and crews and all those who have worked for the success of my journey.

Raising my grateful heart again to the Lord and thanking Him for the successful completion of this most recent pastoral effort, which I hope will contribute to peace and fraternal solidarity among the people of Europe, I bless from the depths of my heart all you who are present, the Eternal City, and beloved Italy.

PRAYER TO THE VIRGIN OF ALTÖTTING

Here follows the text of the prayer composed by the Holy Father, addressed to Our Lady of Graces of Altötting, and read in the Shrine of Altötting at the Pope's express wish on the day of the liturgical Solemnity of the Immaculate Conception.

I greet you, Mother of Graces of Altötting!

1. For some days, my way as a pilgrim has brought me to Germany, a country rich in history, following in the footsteps of Christianity, which had already arrived here in the time of the Romans. Saint Boniface, the apostle of the Germans, spread the Christian faith successfully among the young populations and sealed his own missionary work with martyrdom.

My step is rapid, the program of the pilgrimage is full, and so I am not able to visit all those places where I would have liked to go because of their historical importance and the desire of my heart. There are so many important and outstanding places!

Today, when I have the privilege of stopping for a few hours here at Altötting, I recognize again that the ways of my present pilgrimage also are connected with profession of the Faith, which is the main task of Peter and his Successors. When I proclaim Christ, the

Son of the living God, "God from God," "Light from Light," "of the same substance as the Father," at that moment I profess with the whole Church that He became man through the Holy Spirit and was born of the Virgin Mary. Your name, Mary, is indissolubly connected with His name. Your call and your "yes" belong inseparably, therefore, from that moment onwards, to the mystery of the Incarnation.

2. With the whole Church I profess and proclaim that Jesus Christ in this mystery is the only mediator between God and man: for His Incarnation brought to Adam's sons, who are subjected to the power of sin and of death, redemption and justification. At the same time I am deeply convinced no one has been called to participate so deeply as you, the Mother of the Redeemer, in this immense and extraordinary mystery; and no one is better able than you alone, Mary, to let us penetrate this mystery more easily and clearly, we who announce it and form a part of it.

I have lived for a long time in this certainty of faith. With this conviction I began right from the beginning on my pilgrim way as Bishop of that local Church which the apostle Peter founded in Rome, and whose particular task has always been, and still is today, to serve "communio," that is, the unity in love of the individual local Churches and of all brothers and sisters in Christ.

With the same certainty I have come here today, before your shrine at Altötting, Mother of Graces, surrounded by the veneration and love of so many believers in Germany and in Austria, as well as in other German-speaking countries. Allow me to strengthen this conviction again and to recite this prayer before you.

3. Here too, O our Mother, I wish to entrust the Church to you, because you were present in the Upper Room when the Church openly proclaimed herself with the descent of the Holy Spirit on the Apostles. Today I entrust to you particularly the Church which has existed for many centuries in this country and which represents a large community of believers among peoples who speak the same language. I commend to you, Mother, the whole history of this Church and its tasks in the world of today: its numerous initiatives and its tireless service for all the inhabitants of the country, as well as for so many communities and Churches in the world, to which the Christians of Germany send aid so willingly and generously.

Mary, you who are blessed since you believed (cf. Lk. 1:45), I entrust to you what seems to be the most important thing in the service of the Church in this country: its powerful witness of faith before the new generation of men and women of this people, in the light of growing materialism and religious indifference. May this witness always speak with the clear words of the Gospel and thus find access to hearts, particularly to those of the young generation. May it attract the young and make them eager for a life according to the image of the "new man" and for the various services in the vineyard of the Lord.

4. Mother of Christ, who before His Passion prayed: "Father...that they may all be one" (Jn. 17:11, 21), how closely connected is my way through German land, precisely this year, with the deep and humble longing for unity among Christians, who have been divided since the 16th century! Can anyone desire more deeply than you that Christ's prayer in

the Upper Room should come true? And if we ourselves must recognize that we shared responsibility for the division, and today pray for a new unity in love and in truth, could we not hope that you, Mother of Christ, will pray together with us? Could we not hope that the fruit of this prayer will in due time be the gift of that "fellowship of the Holy Spirit" (2 Cor. 13:14), which is essential "so that the world may believe" (Jn. 17:21)?

To you, Mother, I entrust the future of faith in this ancient Christian country; and mindful of the sufferings of the last terrible war, which inflicted such deep wounds especially on the peoples of Europe, I entrust the peace of the world to you. May there arise among these peoples a new order, based on full respect for the rights of every single nation and of every individual in his nation, a really moral order, in which the peoples will be able to live together as in a family through the due balance of justice and freedom.

I address this prayer to you, Queen of Peace and Mirror of Justice, I, John Paul II, Bishop of Rome and Successor of St. Peter, and I leave it to your shrine in Altötting in lasting memory. Amen.

Altötting, November 18, 1980
Ioannes Paulus PP. II

FEATURES OF
THE CHURCH'S MISSION
IN GERMANY

At the general audience on Wednesday, November 26, the first since his pilgrimage to Germany, the Holy Father delivered the following address.

Beloved in Christ!

1. It is my wish to sum up in today's audience the pastoral journey which took me, from November 15 to 19, through the lands of the Federal Republic of Germany, that is, to Cologne, Bonn, Osnabrück, Mainz, Fulda, Altötting and Munich. In this way I tried to respond to the invitation which the Archbishop of Cologne, Cardinal Joseph Höffner, had addressed to me some time before, on the occasion of the 700th anniversary of the death of St. Albert the Great. The Cardinals of Mainz and Munich, and the whole German Episcopate, had also joined in his invitation. I then wish to emphasize with gratitude that the invitation which came from the Church was accompanied also by the one extended to me by the Federal President *(Bundespräsident)*. In this connection I wish to add that I greatly appreciated the President's presence at the moments of my arrival and my departure, and also the possibility of my meeting with him, with the Federal Chancellor *(Bundeskanzler)* and

with the representatives of the state authorities, in the evening of November 15, in Brühl Castle.

STRICTLY PASTORAL

2. The strictly pastoral character and program of the visit enabled me—in spite of the brief space of time—to touch upon a series of key problems connected with the life and mission of the Church in Germany. It is well known how ancient the history of Christianity is in that land that lies north of the Alps, on the banks of the Rhine, a history that goes back to ancient Roman times.

And on this ancient foundation the history, properly speaking, of the Church in Germany already fully begins after the migrations of peoples, precisely among those new peoples who previously were still pagans. The beginning of evangelization in their midst is linked with the name of the great Benedictine missionary, St. Boniface, bishop and martyr, at whose tomb we prayed together at Fulda, where was held the meeting with the whole Conference of the German Episcopate, and also with the priests, deacons and seminarians gathered there from all the dioceses, as well as with the collaborators in pastoral work and representatives of the lay apostolate, which is splendidly organized. This apostolate is wide open to the needs of the Church and of society in the various countries and continents, as is testified by the worldwide missionary and charitable organizations, "Missio," "Adveniat," "Misereor." The offerings collected on the occasion of my visit in Germany were destined for the Sahel countries, afflicted by the scourge of drought.

ST. ALBERT THE GREAT

3. The development of the medieval Church in Germanic lands began from the time of St. Boniface, that is, from the 8th century. In the 10th and 11th centuries, that Church gave the Apostolic See six Popes; it also gave many saints and scholars, both men and women, in the courts of emperors as well as in convents and abbeys. One of them is precisely St. Albert, the only one of the medieval theologians whom history dubbed "the Great." Born at Lauingen, he was, as theologian, the teacher of St. Thomas Aquinas, and has great merits in the problem of the harmonizing between natural sciences, Aristotelian philosophy, and the knowledge drawn from the Word of divine Revelation. He came to the end of his life as Bishop of Ratisbon in Cologne seven hundred years ago. Venerating the memory of that great son of St. Dominic, it was impossible not to recall the great Duns Scotus, who also rests in Cologne, in the church of the Franciscans; and, in the same church, another personality as well: the figure of the great pastor and social activist, Reverend Adolph Kolping, whose work remains and continues to develop in Germany and also beyond its boundaries.

Together with St. Albert the Great, there opens up before us a great historical perspective of science and culture, in which the contribution of the German nation and Church, in the past and nowadays, is enormous. And therefore there was the excellent opportunity for me, in the splendid cathedral of Cologne, to speak to scientists—gathered in large numbers—professors and students, on the subject of the fundamental problem of the mutual relations between science and faith in the modern context. Another meeting, a rather similar one, took place on the last day of the journey at Munich: it gathered in the *Herkules-Saal* some thousands of artists, men of culture and also representatives of the so-called mass culture, which is developed with the help of the modern media of social communication: the press, radio and television.

In the context of the anniversary of the great 13th-century theologian, there could not fail to take place, obviously, at least one meeting with the representatives of the professors of the numerous theological faculties and ecclesiastical universities of Germany, and this took place at Altötting, on November 18.

ANNIVERSARY
OF THE *CONFESSIO AUGUSTANA*

4. Moving along the highways of history, we arrive at the 16th century, at the appearance of Martin Luther and the times of the Reformation. Precisely in the current year there occurs the 450th anniversary of the date with which the famous *Confessio Augustana* (1530) is connected. And although the efforts made then to maintain the unity of the Church did not yield the expected results, the anniversary of the *Confessio Augustana* became for me a particular reason to be present, precisely in this year, in the country of the Reformation, and seek the opportunity for a meeting with the representatives of the German Evangelical Church (EKD) and of the other Christian Churches and communities with which the Catholic Church is in relations of ecumenical cooperation. I consider par-

ticularly important the meeting with representatives of the German Evangelical Church, due to the above-mentioned historical circumstances, and naturally also because of the further development of the whole action to be carried out for the union of Christians, in which we all see the will of our Lord.

This is the way on which we can no longer turn our backs; but we must always go forward, not desisting from prayer and interior conversion, and adapting our conduct in the light of the Holy Spirit, who alone can bring it about that the whole work will be accomplished together in love and truth. It is a work of vital importance for the credibility of our Christian witness: "So that the world may believe...." Christ prayed to the Father for His disciples, "that they may all be one" (Jn. 17:21).

The ecumenical meetings took place at Mainz. The meeting with the representatives of the Jewish community, which had a particular significance and an extraordinary eloquence, was also added—likewise at Mainz.

The pastoral completion of this ecumenical chapter of the whole program was also the visit to Osnabrück, and the concelebration and meeting with the Catholic "diaspora" of North Germany, a very necessary and meaningful experience.

A PARTICULAR WITNESS
AND ENDURANCE

5. The Church in Germany finds itself up against the great tasks of evangelization, connected with the situation of the division of society, as a result of the

Second World War, into two separate German states. These are the typical tasks of a highly industrialized society on the plane of economy and civilization, subject, at the same time, to intense processes of secularization. Under such circumstances, the mission of the Church, not an easy one, calls for particular maturity of the truth preached, and such a power of love that is capable of overcoming the indifference and actual absence of many people in the community of believers.

The experiences of those few intense days enable us to deduce that the Church in Germany is trying to set against those growing difficulties the power and consistency of the faith of those who understand and confess their Christianity "in work and in truth." Those meetings had precisely this eloquence for me, leading as they did, in a way, to the living profile of the society of the People of God. I have in mind the Holy Mass for spouses and families at the *Butzweilerhof*, in Cologne; then the meetings, similar in character, with the world of work during the Holy Mass at Mainz in memory of Bishop Ketteler, the great spokesman of the social cause; finally the Holy Mass for the young at Munich, in the *Theresienwiese*.

It should be added that these liturgical meetings took place in unfavorable weather, in the rain and cold of November at Cologne and Mainz, and with the penetrating cold and wind at Munich. Not only did the participants remain in their places in those difficult weather conditions, but they had already been waiting there for several hours before the beginning of Mass, praying, singing, and meditating on the Word of God. By so doing, they bore a particular witness of faith and patient perseverance.

In the Federal Republic of Germany there are many foreign workers, both Christians and Moslems. The meetings with them took place at Mainz Cathedral; the following groups were present: Turkish, Italian, Spanish, Croat and Slovene; and, separately, a group of Poles and others. The two meetings with the faithful of the federal capital in the *"Münsterplatz"* of Bonn, and with the elderly in the *"Liebfrauendom"* at Munich, were moments of particular human warmth and brotherly and Christian communion.

GRATEFUL TO ALL

6. I wish to dedicate the last point of this note to the visit to the Marian sanctuary at Altötting, in the territory of Bavaria (diocese of Passau), where there had been invited, above all, the female and male religious congregations. At the same time, many pilgrims had come from different parts, especially from Bavaria and Austria. The prayer that I have already written, after my return to Rome, refers to this meeting.

Certainly the severe November weather did not favor the whole pilgrimage externally, and yet I thank God for having been able to carry it out, and precisely under such conditions.

And I thank all the people who contributed to it in any way and took part in it in any way. *Vergelt's Gott* (May God reward them).

INDEX

Daughters of St. Paul

IN MASSACHUSETTS
  50 St. Paul's Ave. Jamaica Plain, Boston, MA 02130;
    617-522-8911; 617-522-0875;
  172 Tremont Street, Boston, MA 02111; **617-426-5464;**
    617-426-4230
IN NEW YORK
  78 Fort Place, Staten Island, NY 10301; **212-447-5071**
  59 East 43rd Street, New York, NY 10017; **212-986-7580**
  7 State Street, New York, NY 10004; **212-447-5071**
  625 East 187th Street, Bronx, NY 10458; **212-584-0440**
  525 Main Street, Buffalo, NY 14203; **716-847-6044**
IN NEW JERSEY
  Hudson Mall — Route 440 and Communipaw Ave.,
    Jersey City, NJ 07304; **201-433-7740**
IN CONNECTICUT
  202 Fairfield Ave., Bridgeport, CT 06604; **203-335-9913**
IN OHIO
  2105 Ontario St. (at Prospect Ave.), Cleveland, OH 44115; **216-621-9427**
  25 E. Eighth Street, Cincinnati, OH 45202; **513-721-4838**
IN PENNSYLVANIA
  1719 Chestnut Street, Philadelphia, PA 19103; **215-568-2638**
IN FLORIDA
  2700 Biscayne Blvd., Miami, FL 33137; **305-573-1618**
IN LOUISIANA
  4403 Veterans Memorial Blvd., Metairie, LA 70002; **504-887-7631;**
    504-887-0113
  1800 South Acadian Thruway, P.O. Box 2028, Baton Rouge, LA 70821
    504-343-4057; 504-343-3814
IN MISSOURI
  1001 Pine Street (at North 10th), St. Louis, MO 63101; **314-621-0346;**
    314-231-1034
IN ILLINOIS
  172 North Michigan Ave., Chicago, IL 60601; **312-346-4228;**
    312-346-3240
IN TEXAS
  114 Main Plaza, San Antonio, TX 78205; **512-224-8101**
IN CALIFORNIA
  1570 Fifth Avenue, San Diego, CA 92101; **714-232-1442**
  46 Geary Street, San Francisco, CA 94108; **415-781-5180**
IN HAWAII
  1143 Bishop Street, Honolulu, HI 96813; **808-521-2731**
IN ALASKA
  750 West 5th Avenue, Anchorage AK 99501; **907-272-8183**
IN CANADA
  3022 Dufferin Street, Toronto 395, Ontario, Canada
IN ENGLAND
  57, Kensington Church Street, London W. 8, England
IN AUSTRALIA
  58 Abbotsford Rd., Homebush, N.S.W., Sydney 2140, Australia